RICHARD

By

Mariam Ghose Sherar

ISBN: 0-7596-9265-3 (softcover)
ISBN: 0-7596-9264-5 (ebook)

This book is printed on acid free paper.

1stBooks - rev. 3/21/02

Part 1

Mariam Ghose Sherar

Part 1

Mariam Ghose Sherar

He was just a youth I met, one of the hundreds of young men who, unhappy with their lives, families or themselves, have taken to the streets and have become part of the "homeless" culture.

I do not know why I was attracted to him. I am a grandmother of three normal, healthy and relatively sane boys. They live some distance away, and I do not get to meet them often, but when I do I am grateful that they seem happy and active, enjoying their life-style and feel truly blessed because of its richness.

Maybe that is why I felt so drawn to Richard. I had so much. He had nothing. I had so much love to give. He needed loving.

Richard was homeless. There was a record of poverty abuse, and cruelty in his family. Poverty, abuse, homelessness, these tend to build up within a person a hard exterior defense system. Even though one's inner self may yearn for a home, love and security, there is always fear. So, as was true with Richard and so many like him, he rejected any overtures toward friendship. The real fear was of getting hurt again, of having to bear even more pain than one was already carrying. The gruff exterior would not allow acceptance of kindness.

According to Richard, kindness itself, was regarded as 'do-goodness'.

'You are better than I am'

'You get 'points' in heaven by doing good to someone.'

'It helps you get rid of your guilt, because of where you are and I am here.'

'No way.'

'Go away'.

'Don't interfere with my life.'

'Don't try to control me.'

'Don't superimpose your life-style upon me.'

'Don't poor you me'.

Implicit in all of these statements was the recognition of inequality.

How does one reach such a youth? How does one explain that 'all of the above' does not apply in this case? How does one explain that love and kindness are not always given as points? How does one explain that all relationships are not sexual or abusive? How does one explain that an age difference, although it exists, is not necessarily constrictive?

Initially Richard came to me as a "Jack of all Trades". He was a boy whose offer to do yard work or odd jobs around the house was very much appreciated. We began our friendship slowly, two steps forward, one step back. In a way he reminded me of a cat I once had. A stray. She meowed at the door one day and when I opened it, she tentatively put two paws on the threashold, then did her little dance. Back off, come forward, back off, come forward, until she was through the door and into my and later her, home. We shared a relationship, Princess Cat and I, for twelve years.

Richard was like that. I had no idea where he lived, or how he lived his life. But, from the little he told me, he was a nomad, living in shelters, moving on, with few friends of lasting years, and no family to speak of.

He was a nice looking youth, between nineteen and teenty years old, with curly brown hair and brown eyes. He was tall and lanky, and, considering his life-style, cleanly dressed.

He would come to the door, ask for work, and once the job was done, disappear for weeks or months, until one day, he would show up again.

When he worked for me, he would share some of his feelings over a cup of coffee, a sandwich, or some fruit. Thus I knew he was homeless. Thus I knew he had no contact with his family. Thus I knew how lonely he was.

Gradually he began to let down his defenses. He was able to joke and tease. He would play with the cats, especially Hank, whom he adored. Once or twice he would bring me a little gift, a duck he had carved from a bit of wood, some flowers he had picked.

I came to look forward to his visits. I came to regard him as the son I never had.

Then I noticed that Richard's visit became less frequent. Often when he came he would be smelling of beer. At those times his speech was less coherent. He was never abusive to me. But, visibly drunk.

One day, there was a knock on my door, and when I opened it, there were two policemen supporting Richard. who was handcuffed. His whole appearance suggested beligerence.

I was told that Richard had been in a brawl, had assaulted someone and destroyed property. He was being held on a Drunk and Disorderly charge. For some reason he had asked the officers to bring him to me.

I looked at him, my son that never was. He could not meet my eyes. Shame, humiliation, fear, hurt, were mirrored in his eyes and stance. But, he had asked to be brought to me. Could this be a sign of a crack in his 'street-smart' armor.?

I ached for him. Ached to hold him in my arms and comfort him, as I would a child. I wanted to care for him, help him to heal and maybe change just a little.

"Richard" I asked "Why have you come here?"

5

His answer was a murmer so low I could not make it out, but it sounded like 'I need help'.

"Richard" I asked again "Do you want to stay here?"

His reply, again, sounded like 'I don't know'.

I then continued.

"If you stay here you can help me care for the cats, and, if you stay here, maybe we can find out how you can help yourself. Maybe you can go to college. Maybe you can get a job. You can have a home and food to eat. If you want to stay here, I'd like you to."

There was no reply.

Then I turned to the officers.

"Release him" I told them, "Loose his handcuffs"

"He will run away" they said "He will run."

But they did loose his hands as I had requested.

Then I spoke to Richard.

"You have a choice. You can walk away and live the life you have been living. You can get drunk on beer, or worse."

And, I continued.

"Or, you can stay here. Stay with me. It will be a hard pull. I don't want you to change the person you are deep down, but would like to help you re-do those things that need re-doing. You can start to lead a life again with me. Maybe we can break through your past. There will never be abuse again, but I can't promise you that we won't fight, or have quarrels, or have a hard time together."

I added.

"But, the choice is yours. Walk away. They will not stop you. Or stay."

And I waited for an answer.

He stood there. Through his alcoholic beery haze he realized that his arms hung down now, and, though the officers still stood on either side of him, he was standing free.

His arms ached. And his shoulders, where the handcuffs had pulled them back. It was only one of the many aches he had.

His bruises hurt, from his most recent fight, to those in the past. His back was scarred from the beatings of his childhood, and his soul was scarred from the failures of his life.

For the past nineteen years he had been running, fleeing from the ghosts which followed him as he ran. From somewhere in the past came a phrase he had heard at an A.A. meeting.

"There is no such thing as a geographical cure."

It had been one of those rare times when he had made some attempt to get rid of his need for beer. It had not worked. Yet he remembered the phrase.

Running for him symbolized freedom. Freedom to be himself. freedom to live, or die, as he wished. And, as he stood there, flanked by officers on either side, he realized that he was free to run again if he wished. As he stood there he knew that she had told them to release him, to unlock the handcuffs. She had told him he was free to go off, if he wished.

Yet, something had made him tell the officers to bring him to her in the first place. Some inner sense of survival. He was free to go, or free to stay. If he went, he would be free to sink deeper and deeper into the quagmire, if he stayed, free to try once more for life.

He had tried to do so many times. Over and over and over..And each time he had failed. The A.A. venture had been one such attempt. But those times he had been alone. No mother-grandmother-woman figure to stand by and give him the emotional support he needed.

As he stood there, he realized that he desperately needed to urinate, and also to throw up the beer, which had been his source of food for many days. And, at the same time, he realized that he desperately needed a beer to calm him down.

If he walked away he could go to the nearest bar and in the company of people like himself, feel safe for a few hours. If he walked away he would be free to fail again.

Somehow he knew she would not be there another time to offer him a second chance.

So he stood there, hurting, painfully feeling each scar, real and emotional, barely able to stand, staggering in his sickness, still flanked by the officers who stood on either side of him.

He was dimly aware that she was also there, silent, waiting for his answer.

And then, a miracle happened. Out of the open door bounded a cat, Hank, his favorite of the four. He came running to Richard, and in one flying leap, which nearly knocked Richard over, threw himself against the boy's chest. His hands came around to support the cat, which he cradled in his arms, and Hank, purring loudly, kneaded his chest and nibbled on his ear.

Never had Richard experienced such love. Never had he known that he could love also. Because he knew, in that moment, that he could love and be loved. And, if he could love a cat, then he could love a home, and other people, and a career, and maybe even the mother-grandmother-woman who stood silently by.

Still holding Hank, silently, slowly, he started to move towards her and the open door, two steps forward, one step back, until he stepped over the threshold, and she closed the door behind him, and he was home.

I soon realized that, once Richard was inside, and home, our problems would really begin. This was one sick kid, not only physically, but emotionally as well.

Richard had not spoken one word to me since the police had brought him to my door. We had communicated through gestures and an innate sense of feelings. Without speaking I knew his pain. Yet, I also knew that I could not take direct action in order to help him with it, or even to make suggestions. Not yet, anyhow..Richard was too much on the defensive for that.

First things first, I thought.

And so did Richard, as he hurried to the bathroom where I heard him urinating and puking almost simultaneously.

What is second? I mused.

Food perhaps. But what do you give someone who has been starving for days and living on a diet of beer? The chicken soup, which I had started earlier, and was now simmering on the stove, seemed a good guess. But how much, and with what?.

When Richard appeared again, I noticed how awful he looked. His pallor was green, his eyes bloodshot, his whole body trembled.

"Food?" I suggested, and ladled a small portion of the soup into a bowl for him. "And perhaps some bread". Like a zombie he sat down, still not speaking, and picked up his spoon. It shook so bad he could hardly carry the soup to his mouth. But he managed. I sat there and agonized. If he were my youngest grandson, now five, I would have fed him spoonful by spoonful. But not Richard. He must not become dependent, must retain his independence at all costs.

He managed a spoonful, then headed for the bathroom again, where I heard him retching. This time when he returned, I gave him a slice of bread. "Wasn't that what they gave seasick passengers at sea" I murmered.

While he played with his bread, I sent upstairs and readied his bedroom. It was a spare, used occasionally when I had guests. For the present we would call it Richard's room. It was across the hall from mine. If needs be, I could hear him if he got in difficulty.

Downstairs again, I noticed him by the refrigerator. He was looking inside.

"Is there a beer?" he asked.

They were the first words that he had spoken to me.

"No", I replied. "Do you want me to go out and get you one?"

I held my breath. Please God, I prayed silently, don't let him drink anymore.

"No", he replied, and sat down again, toying with his bread.

I pondered. Cold turkey is both painful, and can be dangerous. How does one deal with withdrawel?'

When those policemen had released Richard into my care they had said to me.

"Brother, lady, What are you getting into."

11

What indeed.

But I knew, intuitively, that I could not send Richard to a rehab center, at least not now. He was too sick for that. Besides he needed a home and security, not a place where he would be institutionalized again. We would have to fight this one together, and I could see a hard pull ahead.

Richard's pallor had now turned to a mustard yellow, a slightly better appearance than the putrid green, and the bread seemed to be staying down.

Sleep seemed the next priority.

A quiet room and warm covers seemed in order.

Richard responded to his bedroom without a murmer. Perhaps he was too tired to care, or perhaps too sick. He had obviously not been sleeping in beds for quite a while. I explained that I slept across the hall, he knew where the bathroom was. I told him that I hoped he would be warm enough. The bedroom was not heated, but there were plenty of covers. There was a chest of drawers, a chair, a bedside table and a warm lambskin rug by the side of the bed.

I left him inside the room and left the door ajar.

While Richard slept, I sat and made a list of priorities.

I knew nothing of this stranger son that I had adopted into my home.

Did he have clothes or other possessions somewhere?

Did he have parents or other relatives?

Did he have a Social Security card?

Did he have any kind of financial help?

Did he have any kind of medical coverage?

Did he have a doctor and what was his medical history?

The answers to most of these would have to wait until Richard was more coherent and feeling more rested and was stronger. And, more importantly, had come to trust me.

It was odd. I trusted him. I knew he would not harm me, or the cats. I did not think that he would steal or act to endanger. Somehow I knew that.

I knew, intuitively, that the inner Richard was an honest person, and had a good sense of values. I did not want him to change himself. I wanted him to recover sobriety, feel better, overcome his sense of failure and develop the potential I knew was there.

I was angry at a social world which, through poverty and abuse, had taken a young man in his teens and brought him to this breaking point. I was angry with a world which uses alcohol, drugs, tobacco as sedatives to ease pain, but which, instead, contributes still further to the deterioration of the person. And I was angry at myself for not seeing the problem and doing something about it earlier, before Richard hit his bottom. But, I reasoned, maybe then he would not have responded. Maybe it was too late for him to respond even now.

Well, I was in deep now, and for the duration. And so, with ifs and whys and hows confusing my mind, I put out the light and started for my bedroom.

Looking in on Richard as he slept, I noticed Hank curled up on the bed with his back against Richard's. Both of them seemed peaceful in their sleep.

Richard was asleep with all his clothes on. Maybe they were all he had. His pallor was now flushed and red. But, his breathing seemed easier.

We would have to see about clothes in the morning.

And so, the first day of Richard's coming ended, and I crept into my room, aware once again, of how nice it felt to have a son sleeping next door.

It seemed as if morning came before I even knew it, and with it, again, all my thoughts, fears and concerns of the previous day.

Downstairs I performed my chores, fed the birds and the cats. Made coffee. Debated what to do about breakfast and what to feed someone who was recovering from alcoholism and other abuses.

Richard solved part of my problem when he came downstairs. He was still in the same clothes, very much worse for wear, and now his pallor was ash white. He had made some effort to comb his h air and wash his face.

"Just bread" he said, when I asked him what he wanted.

"Just bread. No juice, no coffee, no milk. Just break."

As he ate, I spoke to him.

"Richard" I said" We have to talk.'

He looked up with fear and apprehension. I could almost hear him saying 'already. Is she kicking me out already'

"No, Richard" I said "Just simple things that I have to know. For instance?

"Do you have any other clothes or passessions?

"Yes."

"Do you know how to drive a car?"

"Yes."

"Do you have a license"

"No."

We were talking a mono-sylabic speech-Yes, No, None of the above.

"Have you a Social Security card?"

"Yes."

"Do you have a birth certificate?"

"Yes."

"Do you have a doctor you go to?"

He turned white, visibly frightened and very softly said "No".

"Are your parents alive?"

"No."

God, I thought, it is like asking questions on an application form, and I know nothing of the vital statistics of this son of mine.

But when he showed me his birth certificate and Social Security card, I knew he was Richard Cook, born April 30, 1977, in a town called Bridgeport, Nebraska.

All the time that I was asking him these questions, he sat there rigid, tight, scared and afraid.

I did find out that he had somehow finished High School, and that he had left home at the age of fifteen, living with some Foster Family until he came to Maine a year ago. He knew some old man in Machias who kept his few possessions for him and where he occasionally bunked.

"Let's go get those things" I said, "Let's get you something else to wear."

Still toying with his uneaten bread he stood up, and I was amazed at how tall he was, six feet at least to my five, I guessed. He was standing taller now, not slouched over as he had stood yesterday, and he walked, rather than shuffled across the floor. His hands hung loosely, his fists clenched, and he looked like some robot, rather than a human being, as we walked out to the car.

We got in, buckled up, and as I started the car, I noticed how rigid Richard was. He sat straight, staring ahead, fists clenched, and there was a trickle of sweat which crept down his forehead.

"Don't' be afraid" I whispered "It's O.K. We will come back home again."

The trailer Richard led me to in Machias was barely more than a hovel. It was littered with garbage and debris, and the old man who came out to greet us was bleary eyed and smelled of beer.

"I've known Dicky here for a year" he said "He's a good kid."

Politely I explained that we were here to get Richard's things and that Richard would be staying with me from now on.

As Richard went inside to collect his things, I waited in the car. Five minutes, then ten, and then the door opened and Richard came out. He was carrying a small suitcase and a shopping bag. We said 'goodbye' and left, and a smell of beer and decay wafted into the car as we pulled away.

"Are you hungry?" I asked "Shall we stop somewhere and get something to eat?"

And his reply, again, was a mono-sylabic "No".

So we drove on, stopping only at the Shop and Save to buy a few groceries. He came with me, but when I asked him if there was anything special that he wanted, he replied again in a mono-sylabic "No."

He did look, I thought, longingly, as we passed the beer and wine aisle, but we walked past it, and on, and out into the parking lot and got into my car again. His hand shook as he helped me put the groceries into the car. I was sure he would drop them, but he did not.

I admired his courage, this son of mine. He had made a promise to me, not verbally, but by the gesture of walking in the door carrying Hank, and I could see that he meant to keep it. It must be very hard for him, I thought. Cold Turkey. That is very painful. I could see that he wanted a drink, maybe even needed one, but he would not drink. I was glad to recognize the loyalty of my son, whom I had known as such for only two days.

And so we went home, as I had told him we would. And it was only when the door closed behind us that I saw his fists unclench and some of the tightness go out of his shoulders.

Munching on a slice of bread, he went upstairs, to his room, carrying his meager belongings with him. Hank followed him up the stairs, and as the door closed behind them, I felt myself relax a little also.

I needed more than a 'yes' or 'no' conversation, but, it was a start and hopefully tomorrow would be better.

I was awakened that night by a terrible scream. Disoriented by sleep, I looked out the window. Perhaps there had been an accident outside. But all was still. The moon shone on an empty road. A loan coyotte barked in the distance.

Then I realized that the scream was coming from Richard's room. Hank had opened the door, which was ajar, and was hiding in the hall, and Richard was sitting up in bed, shaking and trembling.

I ran to him then, all caution to the wind, and put my arms around his shoulders and held him close to my body. I had been longing to comfort him thus, since he first came to me, and this seemed the right time to do so. And he did not pull back, but relaxed in my arms, with tears coursing down his cheeks. As we sat there, not speaking, just holding on to each other, he started to quiet down. Gradually his shaking stopped, gradually his tears stopped flowing, gradually he loosened his hold upon me and the sheets.

"Richard" I said "I love you as my son. You don't have to be afraid again."

Under my arms I could feel his back, scarred from beatings in the past, could feel the frailty of his body,

18

starved except for the beer he had been drinking, could sense the violence of his distress.

And as he quieted down, Hank came creeping into the room again and jumped on the bed. Richard reached out to pet him.

Then he turned to me.

Still in my arms he started to talk, not the 'no's' and 'yeses' of earlier in the day, but with real speech.

"Ma'am" he said.

I was startled.

"Ma'am" I said, questioning him.

"It means Mama Mariam, abbreviated" he replied "Ma for mama, am for Mariam. It's what I have always called you to myself."

"Ma'am" he repeated" I can call you that now, can't I?" he asked.

I nodded.

"Ma'am" he went on "Thank you"

And then he began to talk. He told me of his violent childhood. He was an only child, whose parents beat him often, for their own sadistic pleasure.

"They would laugh while I screamed" he said.

They had been killed in a car accident after he left home.

He told me of the foster parents who had taken him in after he ran away from home at the age of fifteen and his parents had been killed. The man had been a doctor and continued the abuse he had run from at home.

He told me of the old man in Machias, who had fed him beer to the point of addiction.

In between he had tried to get away from it. But always he had returned to abuse, failure, drinking. The last time he had been really scared. He had been paraded through the streets in handcuffs, humiliated. He had felt, as he called it 'like a piece of shit'. And then he had thought of Ma'am. He had not thought beyond that, only that, if he could get to me, maybe he might not fail again.

As I held him, I reassured him that now that all the garbage was out, it would not fester anymore. I assured him that the past was over, that a future lay ahead. I told him that we would talk of what that future might be later, but for now, with release, would come peace.

Leaving him momentarily, I went downstairs, and brought him a glass of milk and a sandwich. He ate the sandwich, drank the milk, and this time he did not vomit.

A slow smile played around his lips. I had not seen him smile since he had come to me, and it looked good upon his face.

"That tasted good" he said "Especially the bread."

"Sleep" I said, releasing his body and laying him gently upon the bed. "Sleep" I repeated, and "Goodnight."

As I got up to go to my room he looked up ever so gently, and murmered "Goodnight Ma'am" and I stumbled to my room, blinded by my tears.

In the days that followed, Richard and I began to concentrate more on practical things. He needed clothes. He needed a medical exam, to assure me, primarily, of his health. And, since he had told me that he could drive a car, he needed a driver's license.

We were feeling more relaxed, each to the other, and were experiencing less of that 'walking on eggs' fear of hurting or offending the other.

For clothes, I took him to the Recycle Shop, our local thrift shop.

"You choose, Richard" I told him, "Whatever you want"

He looked at the rows of clothes, bewildered.

"Pants, shirts, jackets. You don't have to worry about price. Just make sure that they fit and are of good quality."

I saw him walk over to the rack, and start taking things off to look at them. He began to put a few aside.

"Make a pile" I said "Here" And I gave him a box to put them in. "Get a few sweaters also. It's cold out."

His choices, although more the style of a teenager than I would have chosen, were good enough. He chose dark, earthy colors, plaids, colors which seemed to fit in with his

21

complexion. He had such dark curly hair. The browns, oranges and reds fit in nicely.

Later we went and bought some underwear, shoes, socks, and kinds of things one does not ordinarily buy used. I also bought him things men usually need, like shaving materials, toiletries, a comb and a tooth brush.

The clothes that we had brought from Machias we threw away. They were worn, threadbare and smelled of beer and tobacco. No amount of washing seemed to help get rid of the smell.

Some day we would have to buy new clothes for him, but that would have to wait for awhile.

I wanted Richard to feel new, and fresh, as if he was truly starting all over again.

Next on the list was the Driver's License. Richard knew hot do rive, but he needed the license.

The Motor Vehicles Bureau scared Richard half to death.

"It reminds me of a Police Station" he said.

But I made him go to the window, ask for the necessary papers, get a manual and fill out the forms. Scared as he was, he did as I asked.

Fortunately there was not a long line. Richard was not a very patient person and he resented lines, or having to deal with any kind of bureaucratic procedure for that matter.

I could see how impatient he was getting. He had such a short fuse. I suspected part of it was his background. He wanted everything now, did not want to wait, even for a few seconds.

It did not take Richard long to study the manual. He knew most of the material, except, perhaps, for local Maine rules.

A few days later, therefore, we returned to Ellsworth so he could take the exam for a learner's permit.

Having to take the exam was also traumatic for him.

"It's only a learner's permit" I told him, "Why should you be afraid?"

I added.

"You know all the material. Go in there and concentrate on the questions. We have gone through most of them together."

They called his name, he disappeared into the exam room and I waited. Of course he passed. Despite his fear, Richard was a bright boy and he did know his material.

When the time came for him to take his road test, I could see all his old fears return.

"Why do I have to take another exam?" he asked, "Why can't I just get in the car and drive.?"

"Bureaucracy" I replied "Bureaucracy. But what if any old Joe could drive a car? I'd not like to be on the road with them."

The day for his appointment for a road test came and he drove to Ellsworth with me sitting beside him.

"Just pretend I'm with you" I told him "You know how to drive."

They called his name and Richard got into the car. The Instructor, an officer, was kind enough. He must have been used to scared youths taking their tests.

But Richard did know how to drive, even to parallel park, and of course he passed.

I had to laugh though. His complexion was pasty white when he got out of the car. I could see those familiar signs of fear, tensed back, clenched fists. But, the officer gave him a temporary license and told him that a permanent one would be forwarded in the mail.

Maybe some day, he would overcome his terror of the police or officers of any kine.

The medical exam was even more terrifying to Richard. Richard's experiences with doctors had always been negative. To him they were 'sadistic creeps who probed and prodded and caused pain'. His opinions were probably influenced by the doctors he had met and accentuated by his very bad experience in a foster home, where the head of the household had been a doctor.

I settled on a nearby Health Center, and accompanied Richard there personally.

I had already explained to the doctor the nature of Richard's previous years, and any doctor who examined him would see the scars on his back, the results of the beatins that he had endured. I had also told them of his addiction to beer, and how he was trying, cold turkey, to get rid of his addiction. Of his previous medical history in Nebraska I knew nothing, but those records could be obtained by the Medical Center if they needed them.

It took all of my persuasion to convince Richard to go for his examination.

"You have to go" I told him "I have to know that you are alright, and if not, what to do about it. You are my son now. I want you to be healthy."

He was really rigid when we entered the Medical Center and sat there beside me, pale as a ghost, and he looked at me pleadingly.

"Ma'am" he said "Let's go home please. I'm O.K Really I am."

I held on to his hand, trying to calm him somewhat.

"If you want, Richard, I'll go in with you to the doctor when you are being examined."

"No way" he said "No. Never mind. I'll go."

They called his name then, and I waited in the waiting room reading a magazine.

"Of course he was alright. Malnourished. I knew that. Anaemic.. I had guessed that. But his general health was good. I had been so afraid that his beer drinking might have damaged his liver or some other organ, but, fortunately he had escaped that.

"He is basically a healthy boy" the doctor told me "I don't know. He must have a good constitution. Really. To come off the drinking without damage."

It was a relief to both of us when it was over. The doctor had recommended vitamins, a good diet and exercise. That was all.

"I feel better now" I told him. "You have clothes to wear, a license to drive a car, and your health is not too bad."

He looked at me as I spoke.

"Me too" he said "But I hope I never have to go through that ever again."

I was astonished, one day, in looking over the things in Richard's room, to find that among his scant possessions were two books.

TWO YEARS BEFORE THE MAST\
THE WRECK OF THE MARY DEARE.

"Do you like the sea?" I asked him.

"I never saw the sea until I came to Maine" he replied, "But now that I have seen it, I like it."

He thought for a minute.

"No. I more than like it. I love it. I used to sit by the Dyke in Machias and watch it all the time."

How could he have known, how could I have known, that of all the lads in the world, a sea-loving child would come to the home of a sea-loving Ma'am.

I have always loved the sea. Ships, the Oceans, anything connected to seafaring, have always fascinated me. When I was a child I wanted to be a sea captain, but, of course fifty years ago, it was not considered an occupation for a woman. But I have all kinds of books on ships, and the sea, and have even written one myself, SHIPPING OUT.

"We shall visit ships" I promised him. "We shall sail on ships, go on ferries, visit ocean liners and cargo ships. You shall smell the ocean air. You shall have your fill of the sea.

At night, while Richard ate his bread and drank his milk, I would tell him stories of the ships that I had been on, starting with the EUROPA in 1931, and the ALBERT BALLIN on which we had returned from France in 1932. I told him about the freighter NEW ORLEANS upon which we had sailed to India in 1936. I showed him the article that I had written about the GRIPSHOLM, the ship on which we had returned to the States in 1945. I spoke of how I had visited my parents in London in 1948 and had sailed upon the QUEEN MARY to do so. That following year, in February 1949, I had sailed upon a tiny freighter called the CONSUELO. We had been caught in a storm in the North Atlantic. I had been the only woman, and only one of three passengers on that ship. I told him of my cruise to Bermuda in the QUEEN OF BERMUDA in 1966 and how, only recently, just before Richard came into my life, I had taken a cruise on the QE2.

He took it all in. I was feeding his already lit flame. Both of us enjoyed these 'bedtime' stories tremendously.

All this time we shared our adventures together. Richard was still wary of being alone, even of leaving the house without me. But, one day, I suggested that he take the car and go somewhere on his own.

"Alone" he said "No."

I could see the old fear again. His rigid back, his clenched fists.

"Yes, alone" I said.

"Do you trust me to go alone? What if I take the car and don't come back?"

"Oh, Richard" I told him "The day you picked up Hank and walked into my home, from then on I have trusted you. How could I not? You have become a son to me. Go. Enjoy a day on your own. Only come back tonight so I can hear about your day."

And he went.

Scared as he was, he got into the car and turned the key in the ignition. He drove slowly, not really knowing where he was going.

At the junction of Rte 182 and Rte 1 he turned toward the town of Milbridge, six miles away. The road ran parallel to the Narraguagus River, which emptied into the sea in that town. The town itself was larger than

Cherryfield, and had restaurants, gift shops, banks. Since it was still winter there was snow on the ground and it was cold.

He turned again, on Rte 1A and crossed two bridges over the river, and then he spotted the Marina. It was closed, still he parked the car alongside the road and looked. In the distance he saw Islands, with the ocean beyond them, only a few miles away. There was the smell of the sea and gulls flying overhead.

It was different from the Dyke at Machias. It was more wild, somehow it seemed more intense.

He sat there in the car, visualizing how it would be in the summer, with lobster boats plying their trade.

It was his adventure for the day. Ma'am had been right. He had to become less dependent upon her. He felt his blood stir. The manhood in him come alive.

He was feeling so much better now. He had good food, and his craving for beer was less. He knew that he had a way to go yet. Deep inside him, buried, were all those years of pain. Sometimes he still felt scared. Sometimes resentful. And sometimes he asked himself whether he deserved this, a nice home, decent food, love. Even this car of Ma'am's that he was driving.

But, scared or not, he felt better after this jaunt. He turned the car back toward's Ma'am's, smiling.

And, while Richard was gone, I thought about him. From day one I had decided that Richard must be independent. We could share a house and love, but we must be free to be ourselves, and not become overly dependent upon the other.

Oh yes, while he was gone, I worried. As much as I did the time I allowed my twenty one year old daughter to hitch-hike around the world. She was as old then, as

Richard was now, and had just graduated from college. If children cannot be free, within limits, then there cannot be love. One has to trust one's child.

When Richard came home that evening he was fine. The car was fine. He never told me where he had been and I did not ask. For all I knew he could have been parked around the corner, and was sitting in the car all day.

But, as he came in the door, I saw a sparkle in his eyes, and a smile on his face. His hands hung free and his fists were not clenched. In some way he had put a demon to bed. He was not a trembling kid or a beligerent youth. He had broken that chain and came into my house that day as a fledgling adult.

My house is old and Victorian. It was built around 1845 and I have tried to maintain the flavor of that period in furnishing it.

So, I have provided Early American pieces of furniture, a Hoosier Hutch in the kitchen, a set of Victorian Sofa, Chair and Rocker in the Parlor, which I call the front room. There are old painted pine beds in the bed rooms, and because I have traveled, or friends of mine have, there are artifacts from India, Indonesia, Spain. I call my front room my India room, because pictures, bronze and books from that country are kept there.

I found Richard in my India room one day, standing before three pictures I had placed on my mantle piece, one of my mother, one of me as a child with Gandhi and one of my father. There was also a portrait of my mother's Guru there.

"Hi" I said "You looked engrossed. What's going on?"

He turned to me with a puzzled expression on his face.

"It's weird" he said "Who are these people? I've never seen people look like that."

"Weird" I replied "They don't look weird to me. Why do you say that?"

"They dress so funny. And they don't look like people I've ever met."

It occured to me that Richard, living an insulated life in Nebraska, may never in his life have met people from India or other countries.

"That picture there" I told him "Is one of my father. He is Indian, and he was born in India. He lived in the States for twenty years. When he was twenty four he had to leave India. He was a political exile. He was fighting for India's Independence from the British. He was a student of Calcutta University at the time."

"I know about India. I studied that in geography class. But, you are not Indian, are you? I thought you were American."

"I'm half Indian. My mother was born in America and she was not Indian. I've lived in India though, when I was young. I was twelve when my father took me, my mother and sister to India, and twenty one when I came back to the States."

"You lived in India?"

"Yes."

He was silent, thinking.

He pointed to another picture of me, standing with my mother and sister when we were photographed with Gandhi."

"Is that you?"

"Yes. That little girl, there. I was seven when that picture was taken of me in 1931 in London. My father sent us there to invite Gandhi to come to this country, only he never came."

"Who was Gandhi?"

"Richard. Didn't they tell you about Gandhi in school?"

"Maybe. I guess I never paid much attention then."

"Gandhi also fought for India's freedom. He was very famous. He believed in Non-Violence. He thought it was better to get India's freedom peacefully, without fighting and bloodshed. In the end, though, there was bloodshed."

He still seemed puzzled.

"You know" he said, I can't see you as being Indian or living somewhere else. To me you seem like an American."

"I am an American" I replied.

"But don't people in India act differently.?"

"Richard" I replied "Maybe people look different, eat different foods, speak different languages, but we are still all human beings."

I added.

"When I first went to India, I was just a girl of twelve, and even though I knew about India and had met Indians when I first went to India, I felt very confused, maybe like you are feeling now. I felt different. And then, one day I saw a child about my age cry, and her mother came and comforted her, and hugged her, and she started to smile. And I thought, that child is like me. She cries. She laughs. She is loved. And after that I did not feel so foreign. Then, once I learned how to speak the language and made friends, I did not feel so funny anymore, and now I love India."

He looked at me shyly.

"Being with you, I feel like you must have been when you first went to India. Everything seems so different. It scares me."

"It is scary at first, until you get used to it."

His eyes kept going to the pictures.

"Who is that a picture of? He really looks funny. And why is he dressed in that funny robe?"

"That was my mother's guru. When she was in India he taught her something about Indian religion and philosophy.?

"Why is he dressed that way?"

"Because he is like a priest. You've seen Catholic priests, seen how they dress. He is like that, only his robes are saffron colored."

Richard was very quiet. I had noticed that about him. As insulated as he had been as a child, his mind was willing to learn new things.

"The only people I know are from Nebraska, and that old man I met in Maine and you, but I never thought of you as different. I always thought of you as American like me."

"I am American" I replied, "Only I'm part Indian also. I still have lots of relatives that I go and see in India. I've been back to celebrate my father's centennial in 1992. But I live here. This is my home.

As he stood there, I could sense his unease.

"It's O.K., Richard" I said "I know how hard it is to understand. For now, just think of me as you always have. I'm still me, aren't I?"

"Guess so. Gosh. It's scary."

I held him close.

"Sure it is" I said. "Maybe some day you will go to India, or travel to other countries. It gets less scary when you travel around. Nebraska and Maine are only a beginning."

"Maybe" he said "But for now, all I want is being here, and I don't want to even thin k of going anywhere else."

He started to leave the room.

"I'll come back and look some more", he said, "Maybe I'll get used to them."

"Of course you will, Richard" I said "Of course you will."

And I gave him a hug as he left.

Richard had come to me late in January and by the middle of March, both of us seemed to be adjusting to the other.

For myself, after living alone with four cats for company, it was odd to know that there was another person in the house.

I cannot speak for him, but I guessed, at least temporarily that he was content to just be.

I was relieved to see him regain sobriety and an appetite. From only bread, he not ate voraciously, any and everything that was placed before him. He was filling out, and gaining weight, and was a sad example of the malnourished report we had received from his medical examination.

I had seen a lawyer and was trying to adopt him legally, and if that were not possible, at least get legal protection for him. I knew his parents were dead, and no one else seemed interested in his existence. But his age, nineteen (he would turn twenty on April 30) to my seventy three might present a stumbling block.

Richard had only been with me six weeks. He had a record of twenty years of cruelty behinb him, and those roots went down deep.

The scars on his back, although long healed, were reminders of that cruelty. We were only now beginning to work on his inner scars.

He was a difficult boy to reach. After his hysterical outbreak, he rarely spoke of his past. But it showed up often. If he was upset his back would be tight and erect and his hands would clench. If he was frustrated he would retreat to his room, and, if not pout, at least stay there until he had calmed down.

He was always gentle with the cats, especially Hank, and me.

Yet I could sense the hidden anger and bottled up emotions that were still there, still not resolved.

By now he had gained the courage to go out alone, and since he now had a driver's license, I would let him use the car, to go to the store, or just for a ride.

By now, also, the community knew that Mariam had a young boy staying with her. They were unsure of this relationship, but I referred to him as my son.

One day in Mid-March Richard came to me with his coat on, asked for the car keys, and said that he was going out for awhile. I did not ask him where he was going. Part of my whole approach to him was to base my relationship with him on trust. Usually he told me where he had been, or what he had done.

So, at the time, the request seemed innocuous enough.

"Be careful" I told him "I'll see you later."

Later that day, as I started to prepare dinner, I realized that Richard had not come home yet. My car was not parked in the driveway. We needed bread. Since day one Richard always ate bread with his meals.

But as the evening grew late and he was not back, I started to worry.

Had he been in an accident?

Had the car broken down?

I knew he could phone if he got in difficulty. He had the phone number.

Maybe I should call the police.

Maybe I should alert the neighbors and ask them if they had seen him.

I decided against doing anything. Policemen were still terrifying to Richard, and there was no need to alert the neighbors as of yet.

So I waited. And waited. And waited.

I must have fallen asleep in the chair, because when I woke up the cats were hungry, dawn had come and gone, it was morning and there was still no Richard.

I can hardly explain my emotions that morning. I had come to love that boy. He had truly become my son, emotionally and psychologically. I did not want to lose someone I had just found. The tears came to my eyes and they would not go away.

But I knew, unless Richard was hurt somewhere (and by now I would have heard about that) I had to let it, and Richard go. I could not hang onto Richard if he did not want me to.

So I sat there, crying bitterly, and letting the tears flow.

And that is how he found me, as he came in the door that morning. I looked up at him as he stood there.

He came into the room, warily, walking slowly towards where I sat. He looked haggard. His body was taut. His fists were clenched. And he was beligerent.

"Go on and hit me" he sneered "Give me hell".

"Richard" I sobbed "You are here? Are you alright? What happened?"

He looked at me again, coming closer. Thank God he did not smell of beer.

"I hate you" he said, "I hate you" and then even more violently "I hate you'. And then he too began to cry.

"No, that's not right" he said "I hate me."

He stopped for a minute, then went on.

"I tried to go away. I wanted to be free. I don't want to love you, or have you love me. It ties me down. I can't be free that way."

"And are you free now?" I asked "Why did you come back?"

"Because I can't stay away. And that ties me down even more. I tried. I went back. But I could not go back. And now you will send me away. And I hate you."

"Richard" I said "Come here" and I was getting angry now. "Come here" I said it as a scolding parent would and I was angry.

He came. He stood closer to me, and he was trembling. I could almost hear him saying "Now comes the beating."

"Don't you ever do that to me again" I said. "Don't you ever put me through the torture of a night like that. Don't you ever hurt me like that. If you want to go, then go, but do it like a man and tell me first. I won't stop you. I did not then. I will not now. But I love you as my son and I was so worried about you."

He stood there. Silent like a stone./Fists clenched.

"Hit me" he said "Beat me. Put more scars on my body" He took off his belt and handed it to me. "Beat me" he yelled "I know I'm a no good fucking son of an ass. Beat me."

I handed him back his belt.

"I don't need to beat you" I replied "You are doing it to yourself". I added "How can I beat the son I love?"

Then more sternly "Now, come here".

And he came.

"The keys are in the car" he murmered "I did not wreck it. I'm going."

He started for the door.

"No" I said "No way. Not yet. Come here."

And he came closer, standing before me.

"We'll talk about this later" I said "For now come here."

And he came still closer. I held his shaking body in my arms close, kissing his hair, touching his face.

"We'll talk later" I repeated. "Now go upstairs and stay in your room until I call you. And for the duration you are grounded. Do you understand? Grounded. You are not going anywhere."

"Yes, Ma'am" he said meekly, and he headed for the door.

"And no Hank" I yelled, "Grounded is grounded is grounded."

He looked at me and there was a strange expression in his eyes.

"I'm going" he said "I'm going."

And off he went. And I sat down and I cried some more. Why did I ever agree to this? I thought. And then I knew. Because love, and whatever hurt it brings is the most important thing that we can have in our lives. And I realized that I had really come to love Richard.

The matter was not settled yet. We had had our first battle and when the dust settled I would know whether I had passed the test.

For now, he was upstairs. The car was outside. I had the keys. No one was going anywhere.

"Come Hank" I called to the cat "Let me get you your breakfast."

Somehow I got through that morning. Richard's door was shut, and he was probably sleeping, so I went downstairs It was time to start dinner. No bread. Of course, he had eaten the last slice a day ago.

"Richard" I called "Come on down. We have to go to the store and get bread."

All was quiet. Then I heard a door close, and he came into the room.

"Can't go" he said "I thought I was grounded."

"You are" I replied "But you are coming with me anyway. Now go and get your coat."

We walked to the car, and the inside smelt vaguely of beer and decay. I had smelt that odor before. I knew where it came from.

Back home, with several loaves of bread and some other groceries, I sat down and called Richard to me.

"O.K. Now talk" I demanded.

He looked at me, sat down at the table and fumbled with the loaf of bread.

"I wanted freedom" he began. "I can't be free if I love you and Hank. It ties me down. So I went back to the old man. I had always felt free there."

"And did you feel free?" I asked.

"No" he replied "Nothing had changed. It was still beer and sweat. But the old guy was glad to see me. Said I could bunk with him whenever I wanted. He calls me Dicky. "Dicky is always welcome" he said. He offered me a beer, But I didn't drink it, honest."

He looked at me, and continued.

"The old guy wanted me to go to a party with him. So I drove him there. Lots of beer, cigarettes and women. It was awful. They gave me a coke and I started to feel funny, so I took the old guy home. I was so dizzy I stopped by the Dyke. I think I passed out. Maybe that coke was spiked."

He stopped for a minute, thinking about that.

"Anyway, when I woke up it was morning and I came home."

He stopped long enough to break off a hunk of bread.

"I came in and saw you crying. Sons don't make their mothers cry."

I Looked up at him.

"They don't? Why?"

"Parents make their kids cry. "he went on "My father used to beat me. He got this kicks when I cried. My mother would pinch me until I cried. I think they played this game 'who makes Richard cry first'. When I screamed and cried, they would laugh."

He went on.

"But I never made them cry. Only laugh. Well it stopped. I ran away when I was fifteen and I never went back."

He bit off another hunk of bread.

"I'm packed" he told me "I'll leave now. I guess I've failed again. You don't want me around here."

"Richard" I said "You are not ever going to leave like that. What is all this talk of freedom? You are not going anywhere until we talk this through.

You talk of love. You think it ties you down. Can't you be free to love and still be yourself? One can never have total freedom. That can only lead to chaos. I think freedom is having the option to choose. You are free to love, or free not to love. You must realize that I love you as my son, and sons can make their mothers cry. Or laugh. Right now you are freer than you have ever been before.

You have spoken to me of your feelings. Honestly. And so you are expressing freedom to communicate. Am I stopping you from telling me all this?

You came in here expecting to be beaten and told to go and 'never darken my door again' but all I can see is my son, who is very confused right now, but whom I love regardless."

"Am I"? he asked "Am I confused?"

"You tell me" I went on "You are not a failure. You have come so far. Do you really want to go?"

By now the loaf of bread was a shambles, with only crumbs left on the table.

"No" he said "Not really." He was near tears. "But I was so afraid that you would tell me to go."

Then he continued.

"If I went, then I would be a failure, wouldn't I. I'd be running again. If I stay, can I still love you and Hank and feel free?"

"What do you think?" I asked him.

"I think, I think, I think I can" he said, and he came up to me and kissed my cheek.

"As a son" he added "I'll try not to make you cry."

He walked over to the table, swept away the crumbs. Then he looked at me.

"Am I still grounded?"

"Damn right you are" I replied.

"For how long?"

"I don't know. Maybe one, maybe two weeks. I haven't decided yet."

"Hey" he yelped "That's a jail sentence. I think I will rebel after all."

"You already have" I replied "Now go. I want to make dinner."

As he went upstairs I heard him ask "Is Hank grounded too?"

"Why?"

He's upstairs and he is on my bed."

"You can't ground a cat" I replied.

As the days got warmer, I started working in the garden. Peas, greens, they were some of the seeds that I could plant early.

I was there one day, fighting the blackflies, when Richard came into the garden.

"Ma'am" he said "It's too buggy out here. I want to tslk to you. Come in the house."

It was too buggy, so I told him that I would just finish this row, and then I would join him.

He was sitting at the kitchen table when I came in, eating his usual hunk of bread.

"What's up?" I asked him. "What's the matter?"

"I've been thinking." he replied. "Why did you say I was not a failure that time?"

"For two reasons" I thought about it.

"You came to me. Something must have driven you to seek help, and two, you fought so hard, cold turkey, to stop drinking beer. People who do things like that are not failures in my book."

"That doctor always told me I was no good" he said. "That I would not amount to anything. That I would end up on welfare or in jail."

It was the first time Richard had ever spoken of those years in his foster home.

"Go on" I said "Keep talking."

"The State put me there" he said "After I had run away from home. My parents had been killed in that car crash. So I ended up in his house. It was awful. He never hit me or anything, but he sure made me feel like dirt. He had a son, Fred. He wasn't bad. He was the one who taught me how to drive. But he used me. Whenever anything went wrong, he'd blame it on me. 'Richard did it' he'd say. When I'd deny it, they would call me a liar."

He looked at me and there was real pain in his eyes.

"He always told me that I did not deserve all he was doing for me. The State gave him money for me, but he used it on Fred. He bought new clothes for Fred. I always had to wear Fred's hand me downs. He never bought me anything new. He once told me I didn't deserve decent things.

He did make me finish High School. I'll say that for him. But he also told me it was a waste of taxpayers money, since I'd end up in jail anyway."

Richard looked up at me.

"Do people always make you feel so low? When I turned eighteen he gave me $50 and told me to go, so I did. I came to Maine."

"They call it verbal abuse" I said "It hurts as much as a beating does, because it hits inside. But, he was wrong Richard. Both you and I know that, don't we.?"

"I guess so" he said.

He was silent for awhile.

"Verbal abuse" he said "You can abuse people with words too, can't you?. If someone always tells you you are no good, you believe it after awhile. Maybe that's why I nearly gave up He was right. I almost did end up in jail."

He came to where I sat, and stood there before me.

"Ma'am. He was wrong wasn't he?"

"Of course he was" I said" But he wasn't looking at the Richard I know, the one I knew was there before the scars."

"Do you think those blackflies have gone yet" he said, I'll help you plant those peas."

Richard's birthday was April 30 and mine May 1, so we decided to share the day and celebrate our birthday's together.

Richard had never celebrated his birthday before, and since he had not, as yet, made any friends, we decided that it would be just the two of us.

We began with a trip to Ellsworth, where we bought a new shirt for him and a trinket for me.

It was another first for him.

"I never had anything new before" he confessed.

He was appalled at the price of his shirt. "$35 for that. Forget it." he exclaimed.

"It's your birthday" I said, "Forget the price."

We also celebrated by having lunch at the Chinese Restaurant. It was another first for Richard. I think his diet, before beer, must have been hamburgers, hot dogs and fries.

"Hey" he said "No bread."

"No" I replied "The rice is their substitute for bread.

"Well next time I eat Chinese I'm bringing bread with me" he exclaimed, indignantly".

I had to laugh. Ever since the beginning, Richard had to have bread with every meal, and often in between. We must have kept every bakery in the vicinity in chips.

On the way home I let Richard drive. He had not driven a car since his escapade and even after his curfew had been listed, preferred to say home, or take a walk in the vicinity if he wanted to go out.

"It's your birthday" I told him, "Go ahead. Drive us home."

Back home I set about baking a birthday cake and Richard went upstairs to put away his shirt.

He came down a little while later and sat across from me, watching me mix flour, sugar, eggs and whatever other ingredients were needed for the cake. It was another first for him. I don't think that he had ever seen a cake made from scratch. Pre-cooked, take-out, fast foods. These were his experiences.

I put the cake in the oven, set the times, and then I called to Richard.

"Richard" I said "Take off your shirt."

He looked at me puzzled, but he took it off and handed it to me.

"Now take off your T-shirt."

He did so, still puzzled, standing before me bare from the waist up.

"Now, give me your belt."

His expression changed from puzzlement to fear, but he handed me the belt, and he started to tremble.

"Why are you shaking?" I asked him.

He looked at me in fear, but he could not answer.

"Are you afraid that I will hit you? I asked.

He nodded.

"Oh Richard" I said "I'd never beat you. I told you that when you first came here"

I reached for his hand, which was cold and trembled in mine.

"But, you are still afraid, aren't you?" I added, "How deep those scars go."

Then I asked him.

"Why did you take off your shirt and give me the belt? You could have refused. Objected. Asked me why"

"Why did you?" I repeated.

"You're my Ma'am" he replied.

"No" I said. "Not that. I think you did so because you are afraid of me because I have the power right now. I have the money. I control your fate. But, you must never consent to brute force, no matter who has the power. Maybe you could not help it when you were a child, but you are a man now, or nearly so. There are other ways to control beside brute force."

He still sat there trembling and I could feel the tension in his hand.

"We are going to teach you Karate" I said "So you can fight back without beating up on someone. I don't want to see you brought before me in handcuffs again."

I handed him back his shirt and belt.

"Go. Put your shirt back on. I'd never hurt you" and then I continued.

"There are three ways in which I'll never punish you or anyone else.

"I will never use physical force. No one has the right to violate another person's body.

I will never withold food or nourishment. I don't believe in that kind of punishment either.

And I will never withold love from you. I don't think that I could, even if I wanted to."

"So, how do you punish someone when they do wrong?" he asked.

"Oh, there are ways" I said "Stop allowances, curfew, scold or try to reason, non-cooperate, lots of ways. But never use physical force. Violence leads to violence and there is too much of that about."

He had stopped trembling now. His shirt was back on. His belt was buckled.

"Come here" I said, and he did.

I put my fingers on his back. "We have to get rid of those scars" I said "Not these. The inner ones" I fingered the scars, speculatively.

"You will have to learn now to stand tall and never cower and tremble in fear. You will have to learn how to stand up for your rights with dignity. And, someday, if you are ever in a position of power or leadership, how to control people peacefully and with respect."

He looked at me then.

"Ma'am he said "I'm not sure I know all you are saying. You scared me half to death back there. But, I know that you will never hit me, and I guess I should have known that all along. I'll try to get rid of those 'inner scars' as you called them, and yes, I'd like to learn Karate."

And then he did something that he had never done before.

"Happy Birthday" he said, and kissed me tenderly. "I love you."

Just then the timer went off.

"Scat" I said "Let's get this birthday cake on the road."

He left then, and I heard him calling.

"Hank. Hey Hank. Do you want some birthday cake. It's almost ready."

I smiled. Part child. Part man. But he is growing up fast.

Ordinarily, this area is relatively free from storms. Most storms seem to go around us. But, on this particular night, for some reason, we were told that a Northeaster was heading right for us. Two low pressures were going to converge overhead, or something like that.

Richard and I were sitting in the front room. We were not doing anything in particular, just sitting there, when the rain began.

"It's raining. Let's check and see if the rain is coming anywhere"

It was not. All seemed relatively peaceful.

"It is an old house" I told him "One hundred and fifty years old and still standing. I bet it has seen many such storms in its lifetime." He seemed nervous, but calm enough.

"It's getting closer" he said "I just heard some thunder."

"When I was a girl" I told him "My father and I used to count the time between lightning and when we heard the thunder. That clap was about fifteen miles away. That one seems a little closer."

It was true, as he said, the storm was getting closer.

"I don't like storms" he said "They are scary."

"I don't either" I replied "But as long as we are inside and dry, nothing to worry about."

Richard did not answer. He looked pale and scared.

"Are you O.K.?" I asked him "It's O.K. Just a little storm. Come. Let's go into the kitchen. I'll make us some tea."

We were on our way, when suddenly there was a violent flash of lightning and a clap of thunder simultaneously. As it happened the power went off.

"Wow" I said "That was close."

I looked for Richard. "Wait. I'll get us a flashlight" I said. Then I saw him. He was standing rigid, paralyzed with fright. I mean really scared stiff.

I went over to him. At first I thought that maybe the lightning had hit him, but it hadn't. He was just stiff as a board and literally unable to speak.

I took up his hand and gradually we made our way to the table. I poured us some tea, then I spoke to him.

"Richard" I said "Can you speak? Are you O.K.?"

Gradually I saw a little color come back into his face, saw his lips open, saw his attempt at speech.

"The storm has gone by" I said "That was the last of it. Drink your tea. You will feel better."

"Can't" he muttered through clenched lips "Can't"

I went to where he sat then, and gently tried to massage some feeling back into his frozen shoulder blades. I could feel life returning.

"I guess that you had better tell me what really scared you so" I said, "That was no ordinary 'afraid of lightning' bit."

"My father" he began, "My father. I was ten, coming home from school. It started to rain and I began to run home. When I was a block away it really came down. Like it did just now. It got so dark, and then there was thunder and lightning. Like now. I got home and the door was locked. I knew my parents were home but I didn't have the key. It was raining so hard. And then there was a loud clap of thunder. I mean really loud. I was really scared. I went around the corner of the building and looked in on my father's bedroom. They were both in there making love, at least I think that is what they were doing. I rapped on the window to let them know I was home and for them to open the door. He looked at me, he saw me, but he never opened the door. There was no place to take shelter so I just sat on the doorstep. About a half hour later he opened the door. I went inside. I was soaking wet. Water dripped on the floor. He yelled at me, told me never to bother him when he was busy. Then he slapped me real hard. Real hard. He told me to go to the bathroom and dry out, and stay there. I guess he had to go because he came up ten minutes later and told me to go to my room and put dry clothes on.

He never opened the door" he sobbed "He never opened the door."

He went on.

"Ever since then, I get like this whenever it rains hard. I keep thinking I was just a kid. He could have opened the door."

I held him as I usually do when he needs comforting, this nineteen year old boy, sobbing like a baby.

"Richard" I said "Let's play a game."

"A game" he sobbed "What kind of a game?"

"A let's pretend game. Let's pretend you are captain of a ship on an ocean, with a crew and cargo and it storms like this. What would you do?"

"How do I know? he said "I'm not a captain. What do Captains do?"

"They are in charge of ships. You know that. So, it is stormy. There you are. What do you do?"

"Are you with me?" he asked.

"No. Just you" I said "So, what do you do?"

"I couldn't let a ship sink. I couldn't let those men drown. I don't know what Captains do, but I guess I'd have to think of those guys first, and do what had to be done to keep that ship from sinking. Hey look, the power is on. The storm is over."

"O.K. Richard" I said "From now on, whenever there is a storm, remember, you are captain of a ship somewhere and you are in charge."

"Now, let us go and finish that tea."

He was reading in his room when Ma'am called him. He liked to read, and he was devouring, one by one, the books on the sea that Ma'am had.

He was also thinking. That storm had really scared him, and it had brought him back to thinking, once again, of the cruelty of his father and mother, and what they had done to him. Talking to Ma'am had helped, and he wondered whether next time, if there was a storm, he would be so afraid.

At least now he had the feeling that he might be able to overcome his fear. He was no longer a child of ten. He was a young man of nineteen.

Maybe, just maybe, storms would simply be storms after this.

"Richard" Ma'am called again, "Richard."

"Coming" he replied.

Slowly he put the book away, and closed the door.

"What's up?" he queried.

"The mail came. Put on your raincoat and go get it for me. My knee is hurting."

"Will do. Gosh it's wet out" he said.

He came in a few minutes later with a handful of mail, carefully held under his coat.

"What's this one?" he asked, handing Ma'am a letter.

I looked at the envelope as he handed it to me.

"My check" I replied "So we have money to buy you bread."

He thought about that for a few minutes.

"You worked? he asked "What did you do? TIIA. What does that mean.?"

"Teacher's Insurance" I said "I used to teach Sociology at Long Island University.

"You what?" he yelled. "You taught in a college.?

His eyes clouded over.

"I used to hate teachers. They punished me all the time. I would come to school late because my parents had made me do something before I left for school. She'd stand me in front of the class. Sometimes I was so hungry. I never got breakfast in my house. The teacher never seemed to care. Once my father had really hit be fore I left for school. I was hurting so bad I could not stand up. She propped me against the blackboard and made me stay there. Of course she didn't know that my father had beat me. That time I could not even get my pants down to go to the john. The blood stuck to them. No one cared."

He went on.

"You were a teacher? You really were? Did you ever hurt people?"

"What do you think?" I said.

"No", he thought for a minute. "I don't think you would."

"But I did not teach school children" I replied "I taught in a college."

"The only women teachers I knew were sadists" he said.

"Were there no good teachers in your school?" I asked "Look at you. You like to read. Someone must have taught you. You went on to High School. You must have had some good teachers."

"High School was O.K." he said "I liked those teachers. But they were mostly men". He went on "But women. They don't teach. They stay home and have babies and keep house for their menfolk. The one's that teach. They are no good."

"Oh Richard" I said "Maybe some teachers are no good, but most are good people on every level. A lot of them care about the kids they teach. They want to help them grow up and be successful. Why didn't you tell the Principal about your teacher? Or about your parents hitting you?"

"My parents" he scorned. They were the ones that told me never to tell what they did. They bet me up, but if I had told the school Principal they would have killed me, really. I mean really."

"Let's go back a little" I said. "Why shouldn't women work if they want to?"

"If they want to" he snorted "Why should a woman work anyhow. It's the men who need to take care of the women. If I ever have a woman, I'll damn well keep her at home."

"We've got a lot of talking to do" I told him "A lot."

"Why?"

"I taught because I went away to college and got degrees in Sociology. I taught because I believe that men and women both should be educated and have the right to a career if they want it. I never in my life slapped a person. The students liked me. My classes were always full.

Richard was listening.

"You should like a male chauvenist."

"What's that?" he really sounded puzzled.

"You.   Listen to me Richard. See whether you can understand what I am saying. The old ways, in which men and women used to relate to each other are changing. A man should see a woman as equal to him, with rights of her own. She should be able to live the life she wants. Your father abused you. He probably abused your mother as well. Is that how you want to be? Men and women have to share life. Men should have to learn to do some of the things women do, women should be less dependent upon men. You and I have got to start now to realize your future role as a man without being a chauvenist."

He looked at me again.

"I don't know what you are saying" He sounded truly puzzled. I still don't know why a nice lady like you would want to teach. Want to take work away from a man."

"Richard" I said "And I was trying hard to be patient, "Look at me"

"Carefully. You and I, starting tomorrow, are going to try to turn you into a person who respects women, understands their equality. We have to get rid of those awful things your father taught you., Do you want to be like your father?"

"No" he said "Never"

"O.K. then. Let's start to make Richard as unlike his father as we can."

I looked at him. He seemed so frail and vulnerable. He was nineteen years old. was it too late.? It is ever too late?.

"If you don't want to be like your father, tell me how you do want to be. Tell me now. Go slowly. Just think it through. Better yet, go get a pencil and some paper and you write it down for me."

He came back with a pad of paper and some pencils.

"O.K. Let's begin. Tell me about one way in which you would not like to be like your father. Write it down."

He wrote "I would not beat anyone."

"Why?" I asked.

"Because it hurts" he said.

"Let's take it further. Do you think that anyone has a right to hurt another, to violate another person'e body or soul. Anyone at all. Isn't that more than just hurt?"

He thought about it.

"I guess so" he said" O.K. Never hurt anyone, no person on their bodies in any way."

"How about another way in which you don't want to be like your father?"

He thought about it.

"He always seemed dirty."

"O.K. How dirty? Only clothes?"

"More than that" he said "He used to smell. Like the old guy. Never really seemed to bathe. At least I don't think he did."

"What else?"

"He always complained. Did you like the food. He always scolded my mother. I guess he also drank a lot. He always seemed sloshed. He always seemed full of hate. He hated me. My mother. The school I went to. The neighbors. His job."

"What did he do?"

"Don't really know. I think he worked as a janitor in some building."

"Anymore?"

He thought. Then he grinned at me.

"Hey, Ma'am" he said "If I change all of that's him in me, will I still be me?"

"Better" I answered, "We've got to get the chauvenist thing out of you. I want to see you as a decent male, who, respects people, does not abuse, thinks in terms of love, not hate, and respects those people like teachers and others who are there to help you."

"Now, come here to me."

He did, as he always does. I held him close.

"We'll work it out Richard. We'll get the father out of you, I hope."

"But we won't beat him out, will we? he said "Never."

"No. never" I answered "We never use violence around here. Only love."

I stroked his back, gently, feeling those awful scars, inside and out, and realizing that both of us had a long road ahead of us.

My plan to 'dechauvenize' Richard (if there is such a word) began the very next day.

We had finished dinner, a pretty good one of pork chops mashed potatoes, salad, and of course the inevitable bread.

"Richard" I said "I want you to clean up the table and wash these dishes for me."

"Wash dishes" he said "that's not man's work. Women clean up."

"Not any more" I said.

"How do you wash dishes?" he asked.

"Look", I said "You have hot water, soap, a dishpan, Now go to it."

"How much soap?" he asked.

"Richard" I said "Just do it. If you run into any problems call me."

"O.K." he said, sullenly, and under his breath "Maybe she thinks I am gay."

"What did you say?" I asked him, "Say it loud and clear."

"I'm not gay" he said, "Only gay guys and women wash the dishes."

"Wrong. Wrong" I repeated. "Gay guys, as you refer to them are people, just like you and me, only they wear different scars. Remember that. Now go and wash those dishes."

Feeling a little kinder I came into the kitchen. "You wash pots separately, dishes and glasses separately. Wash the glasses first so they stay nice and shiny. Dry them and put them away when you have finished. In their right places. By now you should know where things go."

"O.K. O.K." he grumbled, "I hear you."

I went to the other room and started working on a puzzle. It was quiet. I could hear the splash of water, the clink of cutlery, an occasional groan from him.

I could not help laughing.

He came in a few minutes later. "Its done", he announced.

He had washed the dishes and put them away, but the sink was a greasy mess.

"Sink" I said "Sink has to be cleaned and make sure you put garbage in the right bins We recycle around here."

"Slave driver" he muttered, but he was grinning.

He came in a few minutes later.

"Done" he said, "Really done".

Then he added.

"O.K. Ma'am, what was that all about?" "Men and women should share equally in household chores. You should know how to cook, clean, take care of a home later on if you ever need to do so."

"Won't that make me less of a man?" he asked.

I looked down at him.

"Is it still there?" I asked.

"It?" he responded stupidly.

"Yes, it", I said. "Your penis. Is it still there?"

Even though he knew it was foolish, he looked down at himself.

"Yes" he grinned "It's still there."

"And is it still functioning?" I asked him.

He blushed.

"I guess so" he said "Come on Ma'am. What's going on?"

"And is Richard still Richard?"

He looked up at me.

"I guess so" he said "Hey, Richard, are you still Richard?"

Then he added.

"He's more than Richard now, Ma'am, he's Richard plus."

"Good" I said "I was afraid that washing those dishes might make you a eunoch."

'He came to me then.

"O.K." he said It is still there, and yes, I am still Richard, and yes, helping you with the dishes is O.K. and yes, I see what you mean."

"Come over here, you goose" I said.

He came over, as he always does. I held him close.

"I love you, Richard," I said. You are a good son to me. And thank you for doing the dishes.

"I have a present for you, Richard" I said one day. It was Sunday evening and we were relaxing for the evening.

He looked across the room at where I was sitting.

"I don't trust you, Ma'am" he said, "You've got a strange look in your eyes."

I handed him a package. "It's all yours" I said, "I'm taking a week's vacation from cooking."

He opened the package, which included a cook book, $100 for groceries and an apron.

"What the heck am I supposed to do with this?" he said.

"Watch your language" I said, "Cook of course."

"Cook" he said "I don't know how to cook. I never have. Is this part of your plan to make me less macho?" he asked.

"You've got it."

Then more seriously. "Richard, even if you don't ever have to cook, you should know how. They don't call you Richard Cook for nothing. I'll be here, but I want you to plan meals for the week, but the groceries, and cook us a dinner for the next seven days. From scratch, Wholesome, nourishing, meals. Include meat, fish, vegetables, and of course bread."

He looked at me, and I could see that he was visably upset.

"Come on, Ma'am. You've got to be kidding" He looked at me again. "No, you're not."

He thumbed through the book. "I don't know what all these words mean. Braise. Roast. Saute."

"That, my friend, is why I gave you the book. What I want you to do, each day, is plan a menu and show it to me. Only dinner. I'll do lunch or breakfast. I'll help you buy the groceries, stand by while you cook, but you will do the rest all by yourself. Now, sit down, read that book and tell me what we shall eat tomorrow night."

He came up to me. "Ma'am. I can't do that. I've never cooked in my life. And men are not supposed to cook, except chefs" he added.

"Well, it's about time you learned. Keep it simple, Richard, start with a favorite food of yours."

"Fried chicken" he said "I love that. And mashed potatoes and peas."

"That's a stsrt. Now make that list."

66

He still looked amazed. "We'll get the groceries in the morning"

I walked into the othje room and started reading a book. He followed me in, cookbook in hand. "Ma'am" he pleaded "You can't be serious."

"Very serious" I replied "Look up that receipe for fried chicken. See how it's done."

He got a pad and pencil from the other room, sat down, and started to read. He looked up at me.

"Come on, Ma'am" he said "What do you mean, skin a chicken. What does dredge with flour mean? What is a spatula?"

"I'll help you, Richard, tomorrow" I said, "But, you will have to do all the major cooking."

It was a weird week. Monday we went shopping and I showed Richard how to choose a chicken, later how to skin it. He seasoned the chicken in the flour. I told him how much oil to use, how to adjust the flame.

I showed him how to wash potatoes, how to peel them. As we progressed, I could see that he was getting interested. He turned the chicken pieces with tongs, poked a fork in. "Not ready yet" he said.

I showed him how to mash potatoes, the old fashioned way, how to season them, how to cook peas.

When we sat down to eat, he said "I'm a good cook. This tastes good."

"Sure does" I replied.

"Will you wash up, or shall I?" he asked.

"I'll go it" I replied "You are the cook this week. We'll take turns."

"Now, let's plan tomorrow's menu. Remember, you have only $100 for the week. You have already spent some money on the chicken."

"How about spaghetti and meat balls, and I think maybe a salad."

"It's O.K. by me" I said He was a little more confident cooking tuesday's meal, especially since the sauce came in a bottle.

"Only buy lean meat" I told him "Keep salad green crisp." I told him how.

"That tasted pretty good also" he said.

It got harder as the week wore on. He was running out of money and ideas.

By thursday he said "I'd like to try rice. How do you cook rice? Maybe I can put some shrimp in it, or sausage. Can we afford it, Ma'am?"

"You tell me" I said "You are budgeting for this week."

He added up a few figures. "I guess we can afford it" he said "We only need a cup of rice."

"You have to buy more than one cup of rice at a time" I said, "It's always cheaper to buy in large quantities. Anyway I have some rice. You an use that."

By saturday he had used up all his money and he came to me dejected.

"We can't eat today. No money left."

"Let me show you something, Richard," I said "What do we have in this house?"

"We have eggs, onions, potatoes. There is oil. We have some salad greens left. We'll experiment and make a meal from scratch out of what we've got."

With my help we created a meal from scratch, which included an omelet and potatoes, and it was good too.

"Next week I'll cook", I said "And you will do the dishes, O.K."?

He came over to me.

"That was fun, Ma'am. No. We will both cook and do the dishes from now on. I think a man and woman should share this equally, don't you?"

He added.

"That was a lot of work. Maybe I'll learn how to bake a cake, do bread. Cook up some of those Indian curries you make", and then he added "Can I keep the cook book?'

"It's yours" I told him "I gave it to you."

He looked at me again. Came closer. I reached up and he hugged me.

"You know Ma'am. You are really sneaky. But I am glad I did some cooking. I'll try to learn more. I bet I can be a better cook than you some day."

"Don't' bet on that" I said "Don't bet ever. But I think you'll make a pretty good cook at that Mr. Cook the cook" I teased.

"Do you still feel about man's and woman's work the way you used to?"

He thought about that for a minute.

"I guess not" he said, I'm still Richard aren't I, except I know more now than I did last week"

Then he said.

"Lets eat out tomorrow. Give us each a vacation."

"O.K." I said, "You've got it."

Richard was in a bad mood. He was angry because he felt uneasy. There were too many changes happening in his life and he was confused.

He looked back upon his childhood, remembering how his father had hurt him and how unloved he had felt.

"No one ever cared" he thought.

He was getting love and caring now, he should be happy. Yet sometimes even this scared him.

"What if?" he thought "What if Ma'am gets tired of me. What if I make too many mistakes and she gets angry at me. I can't please her all the time. Maybe I try too hard. But, I don't like the way I was. Ma'am says to be myself. Is being myself what I am, or am I doing things this way to please her. I don't really know."

When he got in these moods, he would go to his room and read the books Ma'am had. They gave him solace as well as feeding this craving he had for the sea.

"Someday I'll be free" he thought "Someday I'll be doing things for me, not just to please Ma'am. Or maybe I am doing things for me, not just to please Ma'am. God, I'm mixed up."

Idly thumbing through one of the books, he thought of how, as a child, he had never really had freedom. While other children stayed after school, he had always had to come straight home. He could never play with the children after school.

Still fretting, he went downstairs, and Ma'am was sitting there reading.

"Ma'am" he said "Ma'am?"

"What's wrong, Richard," I said "You look worried."

"Not really worried. Just angry. I was thinking of my school days and the kids I went to school with.

I looked at him closely. His face was tight and drawn, his body tense.

"What kinds of kids" I asked. "What were they like?"

"All kinds of kids. I never really played with any of them."

He swallowed hard.

"I mean I never played Little League or things like that. I didn't care. Who needed it anyway. I had to go home right after school, always. It was a ritual. My parents had had a drink by then, or more maybe. And it was beating time. 'Richard you are late' Thwack. 'You brought mud in on the floor' Bang. I really never saw much of anyone in school after it let out.

There were some Black kids, I guess, around. I stayed away from them. Ugh. Black families in our town. I don't know why they let them live there. The place was bad enough without them coming in. Anyway, my parents hated Blacks. If I had had a Black friend, I would really have gotten beaten.

We were poor, but at least we were white. That helped."

"Black people have scars, too" I said "Maybe they don't always show, but they have scars just like you do."

"Scars?"

"Yes. scars. Why do you feel that way about Blacks?"

"Why? I don't know. I was always told that they steal, rape, you know stuff like that."

"No" I said "I don't know. I know very fine people who are Black, well educated, who are personal friends of mine."

"You have Black friends?" he exclaimed "You"

"Sure I do. And American Indian friends and people from India and from everywhere. People are people, whatever theyu look like outside. There are fine, decent people everywhere. I think that father of yours really did a number on you, and I don't mean those beatings..Didn't we say that we were going to rid Richard of your father"? I stopped.

"What was his first name?"

"Bart."

"O.K. Let me ask you this. Suppose those scars of yours were not covered by a shirt. Let's say that they were on your face. How would you feel about how people would treat you?"

He thought for a minute.

"Even worse". He thought some more. "I'd be ugly. At least I'm not ugly this way."

"What comes through in people, Richard" I said "Is not how they look or what color they are. If the scar was on your face and not on your back, wouldn't you still be Richard? You were not a very nice kid when I first met you, you know. Yet I loved you. Because I knew that Richard was in there somewhere. What comes through is their soul, there inner self. All people love, can be kind, feel pain, have problems. I like to think that when the inner person comes through, they transcend their outer selves."

"More confused than ever, he asked her.

72

"What does transcend mean?"

"To rise above, To go over. Maybe even to overcome. Like you. You are trying to transcend what your father did to you, the scars, your childhood experiences. You are trying to go over them and maybe make you a better person. You are trying to give the real Richard a chance to come to the surface.

Give others that chance also, Richard. Men, women, people of different races or ethnic backgrounds. Maybe we all look different, but inside we are all part of this world and this life. Even Hank and the birds I feed. We are all part of one, everything, all of us.

If you are kind to people, and look beyond their scars, they will be kind to you also, and they won't notice your scars, if you don't react to theirs."

"You got me" he said "I wish I knew half of what you say when you talk like that. I guess it's because you were a teacher."

"Put it in your language, Richard" I said "Tell me what do you think I was saying?"

He thought about it.

"I think you mean that all people, even Blacks, are people just like me. We have had bad things happen to us. But, if we can be nice to them, and realize that inside we are not different, only have different scars, we will get along better."

Then he spoke to me, feeling relieved.

"It's like violence, isn't it? You once told me that violence leads to violence. Doesn't dis…" he stammered over the word.

"Discrimination" I prompted.

"Discrimination. Doesn't it lead to more discrimination in the same way? I don't want to be like that."

"So, don't be" I added "Let's agree that from now on you will try to see people more from what they are like inside, and not the way they seem to be outside. All people, women, Blacks, poor people."

He rose then and stood before me looking very serious.

"Ma'am" he said "You talk too much. You get me all mixed up. I can't think the way I used to anymore. It all seems wrong now. I think that I like this new way better. I'll try. Really I will. But it won't be easy. Very hard in fact. I've lived over eighteen years the other way. You know that. But I'll try."

"I know you will, Richard. I love you for it. It's late. Time to go upstairs."

"Bread and milk first" he said "I'm hungry."

"Bread and milk it is" I said, and we went to the kitchen.

He woke up about four in the morning feeling hot and he ached all over. Not the aches of bruises, but of muscles. He felt as if each muscle was being pulled tight by rubber bands, his sheet was wet with his sweat and his throat was sore.

He knew it was four by the little clock that Ma'am had put on his table. Some day he would buy himself a wrist watch. He had always wanted one.

Lying there in pain, he remembered the last time he had been sick, many years ago. At the time he was a child of six or seven years and it was on a friday. His father had seen him lying feverish on his bed and had told his mother 'he has to go to school'. It was a school day. And they had made him go, even though he could barely walk to the corner to be picked up by the school bus. All day at school he had shivered, but no one had paid much attention to him, and when school ended he had come home again and gone to bed. He had stayed in bed all weekend. No one came in to see how he was. "If he wants food, he can come to dinner with us" his father had said. But he did not want food. By Monday he was still weak, but he had gone to school feeling much better.

He lay there on his sweat-soaked sheets, thinking of that. Maybe Ma'am would not want him to be sick. Maybe she would do as his mother had done, leave him alone to shiver and shake until he got better, if he did.

About six that morning I checked in on Richard before going down to feed the cats. He looked sick to me, lying there, and so I went to his bed and asked him.

"Richard. What's the matter? You look sick."

His face was feverish, his sheets were sweat-soaked, as were his pajamas and when I put my hand on his head it felt hot, and his hands were dry.

He looked up at me. "I don't fee good" he croaked.

He certainly did not look good.

"Let's get those bedclothes changed" I said. "I'll try to make you more comfortable. Can you sit on your chair while I change the sheets?"

He tried. But he was so sick he could not stand.

"I think I remember how they made my bed in the hospital when I was sick" I said, "Let me go and get you some fresh sheets."

When I returned a few minutes later, I had grabbed sheets, some more pillows, and filled a basin with warm water.

"I hate sickness" I thought, "I'm not really good around sick people, but I've got to take care of him What else can I do?"

So, as I remembered, I pulled out the old sheet, put ina new one, lifting his body as gently as I could.

"I know you hurt" I told him "I'm only trying to make you more comfortable."

I added "You've gained some weight, but you are still so light."

As gently as I could I pulled off the sweaty pajamas and softly caressed his hot body.

"Lets wash it off a little" I said, sponging off the sweaty wetness and even as I did so those ugly scars, wet by the water, seemed to stand out even more.

'Damn' I said to myself "How could anyone do that to such a beautiful boy."

The Aloe lotion I applied must have felt good, but Richard just lay there, shivering, and occasionally he groaned.

"Now, fresh P.J.'s" I said "And then I've got to go downstairs for awhile."

He followed me with his eyes, but his throat was so sore talking was difficult.

"It's alright, Richard" I said "We'll get you well soon."

As I left, I could hear Richard groan in pain. The cry reached my gut, and I cringed.

Downstairs I called the doctor, who assured me it was the summer flu, and many people in the area were experiencing similar symptoms.

"Just give him aspirin, lots of liquids, some hot broth, and maybe a little easy to digest solids if he wants any" he told me. Then he added "He should be alright in a couple of days."

I brought him a thermos of beef broth. For some reason Richard did not like chicken soup, although he would eat it, if I gave it to him. I told him what the doctor had said.

"Let's try to get some hot broth into you" I said.

This time I did feed him, spoonful by spoonful. He was too weak and hurting too badly to do it himself. I was reminded of that first day. 'Maybe that's why he does not like chicken soup' I mused.

"Burns" he whispered. "It's hard to swallow."

"Want some soft bread?" I asked "He said it was O.K."

"No" he croaked. "Sleepy."

"Well sleep then" I said. I put a handbell by his bedside." If you need me, ring the bell" I said "Do you think you can?"

But, he was already asleep.

That night, before I went to bed, I bathed him again. I gave him a couple of aspirins and some more of the broth. I also left a urinal by his bed, just in case.

Before I closed the door, I came to his bedside and held his hand. It felt hot and dry. "I'm next door" I said. "I'll be here in a minute if you need me. I love you son. Try to sleep."

He did seem to feel better the next day. He could stand now, but I made him stay in bed. "I'm not grounding you", I teased "Just want to make sure you really get well."

I sponged him again, but when I sponged his genitals with the warm water, he blushed. "Don't worry, I said "I'm too old to seduce you.

So he stayed in bed. He called me later that afternoon.

"Ma'am" he said "I want to read a book."

He was not sweaty anymore, and he was getting hungry. I left him a thermos of tea and some bread. The book I brought him was THE CAPTAIN by Hartog.

"I want Hank" he said "Is it O.K. for Hank to come?"

There was no need to ask. Hank came in. decided that Richard was not contageous and settled down on his bed.

Monday morning, as I was feeding the cats, I looked up and Richard was standing in the room.

"Well look who's up" I said "Are you feeling better?"

He nodded. "My throat feels sore, but at least I can talk".

I told him to take it easy.

"One more day won't hurt. I don't want you to have a relapse. I love you too much to have anything happen to you."

I came over to him then. I felt his forehead. It did not feel hot, and he was looking much better.

"Are you hungry?"

"Yes."

"I guess I know what you want for breakfast" I said, "Bread and milk."

"O.K." he croaked, then he grinned "How did you know?"

Later, much later, he told me of how he had been sick as a child and how his parents had not cared for him.

"Well Richard" I said "This parent does. I hope that you never get sick again, but if you do, we will try to get you well in a hurry."

He came to me then. He was still weak.

"Ma'am" he said, and he could not go on. "Ma'am" he started again. He still could not go on.

"I guess I'm not really well yet. I can't talk right. But I felt so good knowing that I was not along this time."

"Never again" I said "Never again."

It was inevitable that sooner or later Richard and my daughter Farida, and my three grandchildren Kim, Shea and Corey would meet.

I had spoken to her about him, and Farida, being Farida, had accepted the idea of a young, adopted brother with relative clam and equanimity. Kim, my eldest grandson, was only five y ears young than Richard, and to have an uncle only five years older was a novelty to Kim.

Still, I wondered how Richard, my only child up to now, would react to this ready made family of mine.

As Farida's car came up the driveway, I noticed Richard's tight stance, his clenched fists, those tell-tale body language signs of his of fear and anxiety.

I need not have worried. Farida greeted Richard as if he always had been there, and the boys and the dog danced around him, telling him of their trip here, their plans for the summer, and did Richard know how to fish?

That summer we shared a life together as a family. Richard, overwhelmed by so much family must have felt like Hank, and the other cats, who could not find enough places to hide and be quiet.

Farida is vivacious and energetic. When we are together we giggle a lot, we share interests, eat in out of the way places, haggle at yard sales and ooh and ah over s beautiful sunset.

Richard, only now beginning to gain confidence, is much more quiet, and inclined to be very serious. Yet, as a family, once he bagan to realize that he, too, was part of one, he began to relax and enjoy the summer.

One of our planned trips for the summer included a trip to Nova Scotia aboard the Bluenose ferry. I had promised Richard that we would travel on ships-ferries, tug boats, whatever, and the Bluenose was his first experience aboard a ship like this. We had seen ships in Bucksport,, Eastport, Bar Harbor, now we were on a ship of our own. It was only a six hour trip, but in that time I was determined to show Richard every bit of that ship that I could.

We stood by the rail. "Feel that rail" I demanded, "Smell the salt and varnish, touch those granules of ocean salt."

We stood on the deck and watched for whales. The ocean sent up rainbows of spray as the bows plowed through the sea.

"Look at them, how beautiful. Enjoy" I said to him.,

We looked up at the Boat Deck.

"No boat drill on the Bluenose" I told him, "But on passengers hips and ocean going ships there has to be a drill at least once a week."

We looked up at the Bridge. Even the Bluenose has computerized navigational equipment, and although we could not go up on the Bridge, we did look up at it, and the Radar turning above.

We felt the motion of the ship We heard each squeak and groan. We felt the vibrations she made as she plowed through the ocean.

"That is her heartbeat" I told him. "Listen to a ship. She will tell you what to do."

"Its a good feeling" I told him "That feel of a ship, especially when one is lying on a bunk and the ship is rocking slowly."

So, while the others played games, or drank coffee, we stood there side by side, united, as we held hands, and had I known it then, the experience would carry him far and wide on other ships later.

Once in Nova Scotia, we drove around. As a family we went whale watching. As a family we relaxed.

It was hard for us to turn around and return to Maine again. The Bluenose was waiting for us. We boarded her again. And six hours later we were back in Maine.

It was a tradition that Farida and I had that when she was here, we would take a day and go to Searsport to the Flea Markets. It was something we enjoyed. But the boys did not seem that interested and Richard, who was not that keen on collecting, would have preferred to stay home.

He came to me with a suggestion.

"Ma'am" he said, "Why cant I take the boys and go to Bar Harbor with them? I could take them in your car. It would let you and Farida enjoy your day in Searsport."

I looked at Richard, speculatively. He had shown some growth and responsibility lately, but to trust him with my grandchildren, especially five year old Cory, seemed a handful.

"Ask Farida", I said, "They are her children" I was throwing the ball back in Farida's court. Still, I mused, it might be a good experience for him. If it was alright with Farida, then it would be alright with me.

Farida called me aside after Richard had approached her, and asked me that I thought.

"I'd say, lets" I replied "I think Richard needs to be taught responsibility and I know he will be careful while driving."

I called Richard to me, gave him some money for lunch and gifts, whatever, and told him we had agreed to his taking the boys.

"But remember" I said "You are the boss. Don't let those kids take advantage of you."

Farida told her boys the same thing. Richard was in charge. They should listen to him. Not take advantage of him.

They drove off, and we left shortly afterwards in a different direction.

That evening, after we had all returned safely, I called Richard to me and said "O.K. Richard. Tell me how it went? I mean all of it"

He was still glowing. "It was great" he said. "I made sure those kids buckled up, Kin in back with Cory and I kept Shea with me in the front. I figured Him could manage his brother if he got restless while I was driving. And I really drove carefully. I had those kids lives in that car."

"Yours too" I added.

"We got to Bar Harbor and I parked the car. Before we left the parking lot, however, I asked them what they wanted to do. Kim wanted a T-Shirt, Shea wanted to eat a lobster, Corey to look around, so we did all of them.

I just went where they wanted to go. We must have gone to every store on the street looking for a shirt for Kim.

He had a very special shirt in mind. He finally did find what he was looking for. Every darn store. It must have been the last place when he got it.

Corey got bored, so we had some ice cream. I guess it's O.K. to feed kids ice cream on vacation. I was glad they didn't want hot dogs or fries. But they did want potato chips, so I bought them each a bag."

"Farida is a potato chip junkie" I said "They get it from her."

"Then Shea started to act up. He ran down the street and Corey did too. I tried to stop them. They came back and I scolded them. Did I do right? He was in my charge. What if he had gotten hurt?"

He paused.

"It was getting to be lunch time and Shea told me of this place on the water where you took them for food. He wanted a lobster and crabs. Corey wanted a hamburger, Kim and I each had a lobster also. I ordered fries."

He looked at me. "That was O.K. Wasn't it?"

"Go, on" I said "How did lunch go?"

"That Shea. He really dug into that lobster and the crabs. I didn't know how to eat mine, I never ate a lobster before, but Shea showed me. He told me you once showed him how. He got the meat out of every claw, even those little fins. I sort of was so busy watching Cory that I didn't eat much. Then Shea came over to me and asked me for the body of mind, head I mean. I gave it to him. That kid sure ate with gusto. "He paused. "Gusto, I've never used that word before."

He went on.

"We stopped at a souvenier shop. What junk. But I bought them each a jumping lobster. They were funny. And we got some post cards. And I was really broke. But I bought you something Ma'am" he said, and held it out to me.

It was a seashell, tiny, pink, immaculate. "Just a shell", he said, "but it was so pretty."

He paused again.

"Ma'am" he said, "How do mothers keep up with their kids? That's a lot of work. I'm tired. Women sure have a hard time, don't they?"

I drew Richard to me. He really did look tired.

"I'm proud of you", I said, "Someday if you ever become a father, remember this day. Fathers as well as mothers should help in raising their children, all of it, cleaning up messes to buying them lobsters."

Farida came in just then.

"Richard" she said, "I'll take you in as an au-pair boy anytime you want to come to me. Those boys are ecstatic. They can't stop talking about you, and they keep telling me how much they like you" She, too, came around to him, "Thanks brother" she said.

"Like me" Richard said "Like me" He added "No one has ever liked me before. I thought those kids would never want to go with me again. Especially after I scolded Shea."

"You are very likeable" I told him, "And loveable too. Kids don't mind a little discipline as long as it's fair. How about you? Did you dislike me when I grounded you, or scolded you?"

He came up to me. "Ma'ma" he said "You are the greatest. I don't like you. I love you. O.K."

Then he added "I'm tired. I'm going to bed"

And both Farida and I laughed.

As Farida's stay got shorter and she and the boys prepared to go and leave for home, you could see Richard sadden.

"I never had a family" he told Farida. "I never saw Ma'am so carefree. She never giggles around me. She always seems so serious."

"We grew up differently" Farida responded. We've had our ups and downs. My father left my mother when I was sixteen. My mother nearly died of grief. But she recovered. I learned early that there are alternatives in life. One gate closes. Another one opens."

She told me of this conversation. Perhaps I am more serious with Richard, I thought. Perhaps we do need to giggle more together.

She and Richard shared many such conversations. Through her he learned of my past history, the ups and downs of it, and came to realize that all of us, he, as well as Farida and me, have had our share of pain, abandonment and poverty.

It must have made Richard realize that we have scars as well, although perhaps not as evident.

As for me, I have to accept the fact that Farida, and Richard's backgrounds are miles apart. They are very different persons, as my three grandsons Kin, Shea and Corey are very different people and I respond to each of them differently. So, too, is it true for Farida and Richard.

Even the love, and the type of loving I give them is different. Yet, I love them both. Farida my biological daughter, a part of myself, and Richard, my son by chance.

And he, too, has now become a part of me.

I have known Farida for 48 years, Richard less than one. But to each I offer what I have to give them, love, caring, and whatever emotional support that is necessary.

Now that Farida is home again, and summer is coming to an end, Richard and I will go back to our individual life styles.

Hopefully Richard will be going to college this fall, and I will be alone again, as I was when Farida left home to go to college so many years ago.

But I don't think that I will ever really be alone, as long as my family, all of them, are here, and my love is strong. As long as we are centered in that, hear or far, we will share in the emotional well being of all, and after all, isn't that what a family is all about in the end?.

Although Richard had been with me since January, as summer ended, I began to think that maybe we should plan for his future and whether he should go to college or not.

He did have a High School diploma. He was a bright boy, quick to learn. But his past had been so precarious. He was only now beginning to feel more sure of himself as a person,.

"Richard?" I asked him one day "Do you want to go to college? Maybe we can find some course of study at the University of Maine, Machias, that you might like."

He looked at me, scared:

"Are you trying to push me away?" he asked, nervously.

"Of course not" I replied. "I just thought that maybe you would be interested. What would you like to do?" I paused, "Have you thought about it at all?"

I looked at him as he sat there. He seemed much more sure of himself. Even as we talked, scary as it might sound to him, he did not clench his fists, or tremble as he used to. I felt he was ready to go to college, but wondered where, and what he would like to study.

When he looked up at me again, there was speculation in his answer.

"Do you think I could go to sea?" he asked "I'd like that, I think."

I looked startled. "Sea" I said "You mean become a seafarer?"

He looked at me, and there was longing in that look.

"I've always wanted to go to sea, and when you took me on the Bluenose I knew for sure. But I want to become an officer. Maybe even a Captain some day. Do you think I could."

My look must have been very far away.

"Ma'am" he said, "What's the matter."

"Nothing" I said, "I was just thinking. I wanted to go to sea once when I was a girl. Only women did not go on ships then, except as stewardesses, and now you, Richard, want to go to sea. I can't believe it. Of course you would make a good seafarer."

"On the other hand," I told him "It is a career full of pitfalls. There is loneliness.. There are years and years spent at sea with only the ocean around you. There is a bar at the foot of every gangplank. There is danger, both from the sea itself and the ships and their cargo. It is hard to have a family and find a woman who understands. Yes, it is all of that, but, if you want it, go for it," I told him.

I added, "The Maine Maritime Academy is in Castine, and that is not too far from Cherryfield. I would want you close to me for awhile. You could go there if they will accept you."

So we drove to Castine one day, and of course they accepted Richard. I had a feeling that they would.

We were able to get some tuition assistance, and he was able to find a part-time job, and between us we felt that it could be managed.

I don't think that, a year ago, Richard had ever dreamed of going to college. I don't think that he had ever dreamed that it was possible for him to do more than 'odd jobs' or rake blueberries.

And I worried too. He had only been with me less than a year. I suspected that he was still very vulnerable. Could I trust him to dorm life. Could I trust him not to get involved with the wrong crowd, Could I trust him not to get drunk again on beer, or worse. Was he strong enough to resist such situations if they arose.

I had never had these fears about Farida when she went off to college. But then, Farida was not a child who had spent nineteen years in abuse and homelessness.

Or maybe I was just getting older and worried more about such things.

Richard seemed frightened too. Perhaps he was responding to some of my fears. But, as I had determined so long ago, I had to get go, in order to have, and he would have to face his new college life and make what he could of it./

So he worked hard for the rest of that summer. He raked blueberries. He did yard work. He saved every penny that he could. He was a good worker, I will say that for him, he always had been. He even bought a car, just an old Olds, but one that seemed serviceable enough. He needed that. Castine to Cherryfield is near enough so one can drive it in a few hours, but it is too far for a walk. I had to know that Richard would, and could, come home when he wanted to.

That September day, as we drove off to Castine in my car, (his was already there) I felt such a sadness.

I knew that, once a child leaves home, they are never really home again in the same way. Yes, they come home for visits or on vacations, but rarely permanently again.

And, I had had Richard for such a short time. I would miss him.

I saw him safely installed and drove home alone, slowly, carefully, quietly.

A new phase of Richard's life was starting, but a new phase of mine was drawing to a close.

He came into the kitchen as I sat there, looking at early seed catalogues. It was Christmas break and he was home on vacation after his freshman semester at Marine Maritime.

"Ma'am" he said "what do you think about girls?"

I looked up, startled. I had been concentrating on whether to plant Early Girl or Celebrity tomatoes this year, and my mind was on that, not girls.

"Girls?" I answered, stupidly. "What about girls?"

I looked at Richard as he sat there across from me, looked at a lad whose eyes glowed, and whose thick hair grew healthily and glossy upon his head. He was a far cry from that boy who, literally, nine months ago, had come to me in shackles.

"Tell me" I said "What do you mean? There are girls, there are women, there are all sorts in between"

Then I added.

"Are you seeing any girls?"

"Not really" He blushed as he said it "But I want to date, to maybe even have sex with them, to marry some day, maybe even have children."

Women, I pondered, how to talk to this so-recent son of mine about women.

"I guess it's normal for you to go with women, girls as you refer to them" I replied, "But be careful, Richard."

I had to pick my way through this one carefully.

"I know that you have had women. Those first nineteen years must have included some, and sex. And I am glad that you want women in your life, but you have a long way to go before you get seriously involved with a woman."

God, this was awkward for me.

"I think that you have to distinguish between a girl, a friend, a sexual partner or a wife. Right now I would guess that a girl friend would be right for you. A companion to take out to dinner, to go to the movies with, to talk to, or whatever else you want to share with her. And maybe you can even combine a girl friend with sex. I know you are not a virgin. I just think that it is lucky that you never got AIDS or some sexual disease before you came to me. But if you do have sex, be careful." I could see that Richard was listening to me.

"Bodies are sacred, Richard" I said "And sex should be a sharing, not a possessing or a way to ease hunger. You should know that."

"And" he said "And"

"And I want any woman you meet to be equal to you, not some broad off the street. She should be someone who will share in your growth and development, as you do hers."

It was hard for me to go on.

"Richard" I said, and I looked at him proudly "You have had a rough past. You are only now beginning to feel some pride in yourself. Only now are you developing a better sense of self, beginning to develop more positive self-esteem. Maybe you are only talking about girls now, but going with girls leads to love, and you can't love another if you don't love yourself first. You are just beginning to do that."

He looked up at me, and there were many questions in that look. I went to him then, put my arms around his shoulders, stroking his scarred back as I ran my fingers down his torso, and I held him tightly.

"Go with the girls" I said "Have a happy time with them. But, don't get serious yet. You still have a career ahead of you, and it takes a very special kind of woman to be a seafarer's wife. There are long times apart. Sexual needs which are hard to keep in check. And, if there are children, fatherless times for them. Don't get too serious yet."

He sat there, still, and I could see a stiffness in his demeanor, the old clenching of hands.

"Do you have a girl friend" I asked him again, quietly.

He looked up at me.

"It's O.K. if you do" I said "Girl friends are important to have.

"No" he said "I don't have a girl friend, but I want one" And then, so quietly that I could hardly hear him, he murmered "I'm afraid."

"Of what?" I asked "Of what?"

"Of being hurt" he murmered "Or of hurting her. What if she gets too serious? What if she wants more of me than I can give her? Or I am ready to give her. What if, as you say, she wants to be a wife, and I only want a friend? What if I want more and she doesn't? And what if I get angry at her, and hit her, as I was hit as a child?"

"Richard" I said "Life is full of chances. You can't go around for the rest of your life not taking chances. It's O.K. to lay out your cards in the beginning and explain your boundaries, but don't ever stop taking risks."

Under my hands I could feel his body relax, his hands started to unclench.

"Have girl friends" I whispered "Even bring them here. I guess your Ma'am has a right to know who you see."

"Even have sex here" he asked.

I look at him squarely. "Even sex. Long ago I told Farida the same thing. If you want sex, then don't be afraid or ashamed to have it in the open, rather than in back seats of cars, or murky motel rooms. The sex act should be beautiful and enjoyable. But never sordid."

I stopped for breath.

"But remember, having sex should not necessarily lead to marriage. Concentrate of your career first Then think of marriage."

How could I talk so. I, who had plunged into marriage without all this talk and analysis. Maybe it was because of it that I was able to talk to Richard now.

"Richard" I smiled at him "Have girl friends. Just try to keep it clear which is which, girl friend, sexual partner, companion and friend, wife, or all of the above."

And then I added.

"But whatever you do, don't be afraid to bring her here. If in doubt, let Hank decide".

So we ended on a happy note.

"He reached over" Order the Celebrity tomatoes" he told me and "Thanks Ma'am."

The first year at Marine Maritime was a frightening year for Richard. He was alone now, and although Ma'am was only a telephone call away, he wanted to prove to her, and to himself, that he could make it on his own.

It was hard for him to organize his life, so much time for classes, so much time for study, so much time for socializing. College life was very different from his school days in Nebraska. He had his own time schedule now. No father to insist that he come home at once, no beatings if he was late.

Even at Ma'am's, he had felt the need to come home without loitering. Not because she expected it, but because he felt that he should.

He wanted to make friends, wanted to take girls out for coffee, and, if they had apartments of their own, sleep with them. He remembered Ma'am telling him that it was O.K. to have girls. But, he did not want to get serious about any of them. Not yet. Later, maybe, after he had been at sea for awhile. That was, assuming that, some day, he would be at sea.

So the years passed. When he could, he went home to Ma'ams. He was grateful that he had a home to go to. Ma'am was always glad to see him. Sometimes he went home alone. Sometimes he brought a girl with him. Ma'am had said that he could.

The girl he brought this particular time was called Laura. She had red hair and it fascinated him.

"Come home with me" he told her. "I want you to meet my mother, and see where I live"

They had a long weekend, and she was grateful for someplace to go.

"Wills he mind?" she asked. "I mean will she mind that we are sleeping together."

"Nah. She told me it was O.K."

Sitting beside him, she enjoyed the drive. He was quiet, concentrating on his driving, but she could sense his excitement at going home with her.

As they turned in the driveway, he smiled at her.

"Home" he said "This is where I live."

Ma'am and Hank were both there to greet them.

"Ooh, a cat" she exclaimed "Is he yours?"

"Yeah. Well he's really Ma'am's but I call him mine. "Hi Ma'am" he said "This is Laura."

"Hi" I exclaimed, looking at her. She was young, and pretty, and her red hair was aflame. And shallow.

But Laura was not so pleased with the sleeping arrangements. After a pleasant dinner, and a walk outside, Richard took Laura to his room, and Hank followed.

"Richard" she said "I want to sleep with you. Not you and some old cat.

Richard was amused.

"Hey Laura," he said "Which cat are you talking about-human or animal"

Hank did not care. When Richard was home he slept with Richard, whoever was there, and Richard did not object.

Laura never returned. But after her there were others. To him, girls were a symbol of his developing manhood.

And Richard had a nice way with girls. Our talk must have had some effect. He treated the women kindly and with respect, but he was never serious about any of them.

They loved him. And why not. He was a good looking boy and doing well in school.

Sometimes, he would come home alone, and often when he did so, he would talk.

"I'm scared Ma'am," he would say "What if I don't pass the exams. What if I am making the wrong choice? Maybe I should not have chosen to be a seafarer after all. What if I can't get a job?"

"Things will work out, Richard" I would tell him. Relax more."

They were the common fears of youth today. For Richard, whose past was poverty and abuse, they must have been even more terrifying.

"One day at a time" I'd tell him. Let tomorrow be. Concentrate on today."

If an exam was particularly difficult, I would see his old sense of failure reappear.

"Don't hide" I'd say, remembering how he used to run to his room, "Let's face it and see if we can work it out together". And we would.

For me, the worst time was when he left on his summer cruise. But, as he stood on deck, with the other students, in his white uniform, with his curly hair neatly under his cap, I could sense his excitement.

As the ship pulled away, Richard stood on deck, watching the land, and Ma'am disappear. He was really on his own now. The ship was large, THE STATE OF MAINE-and she had formerly been called the USHER. At first it was bewildering.

He attended the classes held aboard and marveled as he was taught about the instruments on the Bridge. He had seen them on sonsuls, but this was the real thing. He loved being on the Bridge. It was quiet, and he could sense how this was the control center for the ship. Someday, he hoped, he would be in command of a ship, and the Bridge would be his domaine.

But, not only was he learning navigation, and ship-board activities, he was also seeing different countries. His ship's destination was Trinidad, an Island in the West Indies. It was a new experience for him also. He had never traveled before. If he had any spare time, he would go ashore once they got there, and explore.

But, he was always busy, there was not much spare time. Working on a ship kept one very busy.

He could hardly believe it, when the six week cruise was over, and he saw the familiar Castine shore line. Ma'am was there, waiting for him, as were the families of other cadets. The pier was crowded with people.

"Ma'am" he exclaimed, as he came running down the gangplank. "Ma'am".

I held him close, then smiled as I looked at him. This was hardly the Richard I had first seen.

He was glowing with health, and as I held him I suddenly remembered how I had first seen him. Putrid green, mustard yellow, flushed red or pasty white. I could not believe that this was the same person. His going to sea had fulfilled, in some vicarious way, my dream of being a seafarer. But, more than that, as I looked at my son, I realized that Richard had become a man now, and a self assured one at that.

It was shortly after Richard's cruise, that he drove up the driveway one friday night, unexpectedly. Ordinarily he comes home for vacations or special holidays, but I sensed, instantly, that this was no ordinary visit.

He came in carrying a bag of bread with him, which he set down on the counter.

"I wasn't sure that you would have any" he explained, "Now that I'm not here."

I looked at his face and notice how he averted my look.

"Where's Hank?" he asked.

I look at him, again.

"O.K. Richard, what's up? I asked. "You don't act this way without a reason."

"Nothing" he said "I got lonely. Maybe I'll take a walk. I'll be back."

Then he came over to me and pecked my cheek.

"No Ma'am" I've got a problem."

"Let's talk" I said "Spill it out."

"Hey. Don't use that word spill. That's the problem."

"Richard" I sighed "Sometimes you exasperate me. Don't talk all the way around the bush. What's up?"

"Beer" he replied" That's what up. Or rum. Or martinis, or anything in between for that matter."

He added.

"You were right about a bar being at the foot of every gangplank. Everywhere I look, or everywhere I go, my friends seem to be drinking. It's 'Go out for a beer' or 'meet some chick at the pub' or a 'beer party in someone's dorm room'. It almost makes me feel like an out caste when I say 'No thanks' to beer, or don't want to go to the pub.

He stopped long enough to open the bag and take out a roll.

"Hi Ma'am. What do I do?" He put his lips against my cheek.

"Do?" I replied, foolishly, "What do you mean 'Do'?"

"Well" he said "I could go and have a beer. Just one./ That wouldn't hurt, would it?"

I shuddered, remembering the Richard of years ago.

"Or, he continued" I could go and order a coke. Do they spike cokes, I wonder?"

"Or" I prompted.

"Or I could make some excuse and stay home. Hey", he said "Someday I'll be on a ship for real. So will those guys. I know that the Merchant Marine is dry, but those guys drink. Even on ships"

He sat down at the table.

"Where's Hank?" he asked.

"Upstairs. Asleep in your room."

"I'll go up and say 'Hello'"

"No way" I said "No excuses. Let's talk this one out."

"Out?"

"Richard?" I asked him "Do you remember when you first came here?"

"In mannacles?" he grinned "I remember."

"Do you remember why you had on handcuffs?"

"I was drunk, wasn't I?"

"On what?"

"Beer. That's all that old guy drank. But one drink?" He looked at me "That one beer does not make you drunk."

"No, but to an alcoholic, one leads to two and three, need I go on?"

"Am I an alcoholic?" he asked.

"I don't know" I replied "But I know that beer nearly killed you, and I don't believe in the one beer theory. There ain't no such animal."

"So what do I do.? Do I stay home and rot?"

I looked at him. I could not help laughing.

"Hey. It's not funny" he said.

"I know it isn't" I laughed "But you look so desperate."

"Come h ere" I said "Come over here."

As he had done so many times, he came around and I put my arms around him and drew him close.

"Be honest with them, Richard" I said "There is nothing wrong in telling people you don't drink. You don't have to say that you may be an alcoholic. You can still go along and order a gingerale. I did that once at a New Year's Eve party and everyone thought that I was drinking Scotch.

I stopped for a moment, remembering that party.

"I used to drink" you know "Not as an alcoholic but as a social drinker, and I drank a lot. Then I met people who were alcoholics. I saw what it did to them. No one can tell another that he's an alcoholic, but there sure are a lot of problem drinkers in this world. I was in Al-Anon for years, I was so confused. You know what I learned? You can go anywhere, bars, cocktail parties, dinner parties, and still have a good time, even without having to drink. As long as you have a glass in your hands, no one really cares."

I was silent for a minute or two.

"I hate to go to bars, or parties, where there is a lot of drinking. I hate to see what alcohol does to people. It destroys life. It nearly destroyed yours."

"O.K." he said "I won't drink beer, but what do I do?"

"Do what you want to" I said "If you want to go with them, go, and order a coke or gingerale. If you don't, say so."

He was silent.

"Aren't there people who don't go to pubs?" I asked, "Does everybody drink?"

"No" he said "Not everybody. I've got friends who don't. But I want to be part of the gang. I feel funny not being so."

"It's only another year" I told him "Soon you will be on a ship and free to lead your own life. There are lots of things to do in port, besides drink."

"Like eat bread" he grinned.

"Why not" I said "Let them eat bread."

He came around to me, and he looked relived.

"Thanks Ma'am" he said "I promise you that I will never drink, beer or anything else. I'll work it out somehow."

And he went up the stairs after Hank.

Richard's four years at Maine Maritime finally did come to an end. It hardly seemed possible that four years ago, no one, neither Richard or I, could have dreamed that he would graduate from college. They had been four years of hard work on his part.

His senior year, the year after his cruise, seemed to go even faster than the other three.

When graduation day came, we were all there, Farida, Kim, Shea, Cory, me and Hank in absentia. Richard's future seemed secure. He had already been assigned to a ship as Third mate. It was a beginning. But we all knew that eventually he would move on, progressing from Third, to Second to First Mate, and eventually Captain.

It was his last night home. He was driving to Boston tomorrow to sign on as Third Mate.

He sat there at the table, biting hunks of bread and drinking a glass of milk.

"Richard" I said "What would you do if I asked you to take off your shirt?"

He looked at me.

"Take it off, I guess, because it probably had a hole in it."

"And your T-shirt?"

"Take that off, too, so you could see my gorgeous body."

"And your belt?"

"No way. My pants might fall down, and I would not want, even you, to see me that way."

He looked at me again.

"Seriously" he said "I know what you are getting at. Those inner scars. Well, they have gone. For the longest time I could not think what you meant. But, really, they have gone away. I guess it's because I like who I am these days. I'm healthy. I look and feel good. I've a Ma'am who loves me. I have a job. And a future. I can take care of myself without abuse. And I now know that I will never let people take advantage of me.

Those outer scars. They are still there. I'll keep them. I could have them straightened out by a plastic surgeon, but I don't think that I will. They will help remind me of where I've come from, and where I am, and where I might be going.

As for women. When I meet the right one, I'll bring her home. I don't need those girls anymore. They were great for awhile. But I need to feel my way now. I am not ready, yet, to get serious about a woman. And I have not met the right one."

He jumped up, looking at his watch. It was a graduation present from all of us. That, and his class ring were his only pieces of jewelry.

"I've got to get some sleep. I'm off in the morning."

He came around to me and nuzzled the nape of my neck.

"Don't worry," he said "Richard will be O.K."

Then he called to Hank.

"Come on, old buddy, one more night, then you can have the bed all to yourself."

After that, Richard came home rarely. Sometimes if he was on leave, he would come home. Sometimes, if his ship was in a nearby port, and he had the time, he would come.

In the following years he concentrated primarily on his career. He shipped out of the Port of Boston, and the ships he was on, mostly Container Ships, carried him all over the world: Europe, Asia, South America.

For a child who had been born in Nebraska, and had never seen the sea, he was getting his bellyfull now.

He made the progression from Third to Second to First Mate after three years. The money he earned he put away for the future, but he also sent me some every pay period. I never used it. I, too, set it aside for a special fund for Richard's future.

Shortly after he made First, he brought a friend, John, home with him. John was a Second Mate on his ship, but they had also known each other at Maine Maritime.

John was originally from Boston, but his family had moved to California. Because he had no family nearby, Richard thought that it would be nice to introduce him to his family.

Richard had always been such a loner that I was glad to see him make a friend. True, Richard was gregarious, but, up to now, had never had a friend in depth.

"Can I call you Ma'am" John asked me, Richard speaks of you so often, I almost feel as if I've always known you.

From John, I learned more of Richard's shipboard activities. He still read a lot, especially about the places that he had been to.

"I get the feeling" said John, That this guy will never stop asking questions and studying about these people we meet. And they love him. 'Where's that Mate?' they ask, "Want to say hello."

Richard was home for awhile while he was studying for his Master's Certificate. It was hard work. His sea time and experience counted, of course. The industry was proud of his progress and so, obtaining his Master's License assured him of his career as a seafarer.

He had fulfilled his dream of so long ago "I want to be an officer" he had said "Any maybe some day a Captain" And so he was.

Some women brag about 'My son the Doctor'. Others about "My son the Lawyer'. When Richard did finally make Captain, there was no one prouder than I. His Ma'am could now brag about 'My son the Captain'. In doing so, he had fulfilled his desire, and mine.

Before taking command of his first ship, Richard had been away on business matters. But he came home the night before to be with me.

He came in the door, and for a minute as I looked at my son, I had a sense of daja-vu. There, but for the grace of God, it could have been me.

He looked wonderful. His white uniform, his four bars, and his name CAPTAIN RICHARD COOK almost brought tears to my eyes. We had never been able to change his name but Cook sounded good enough for me.

"Hi, Ma'am" he said, coming into the kitchen where I was busy shelling peas. "Peas" he said "Are they yours?" He sat down, grabbed a handful and started shelling them.

"Ma'am" he asked "Do you remember the time I ran away and when I came back we talked of freedom and stuff like that? I need you to tell me about that again."

I looked up from shelling the peas.

"Richard" I said "How do you expect me to remember all I said so long ago?"

"Was it that long ago? he mused "God, I must have been a stupid brat at the time."

"Just a crazy mixed-up kid" I replied "Now, where is this conversation leading to?"

"How can I be a good Captain?" he asked. "How can I lead a crew? These days it's around twenty men and women. Yes, Ma'am, we have women on board now.

He went on.

"I'm only twenty eight years old. It's my first command. I don't' want anything to go wrong. What did you tell me then of leadership, violence, power?"

With a handful of peas in his hand, he grinned.

"Captain Richard Cook shelling peas. What would my crew think. Still tied to Hank's apron strings. Not yours.

You never let me tie myself to you. I had to be independent."

"Richard" I told him "Listen to you. You don't need my help. You are already describing leadership. I always heard it said that the Captain's personality influenced the crew's behavior. Someone who is just, not bullish. Firm. Efficient. Calm in the face of danger. Does not take himself too seriously. Can laugh at himself and others. Do you fill the bill?"

"I'm not worried about navigation." he said, "I learned about that in school. And you taught me, long ago, to listen to my ship. And I do. High tech or now, she'll tell me what to do. It's the crew."

I studied Richard's face as he spoke. He really seemed worried. Yet, as he spoke, he was saying all the right things.

"I sailed under one guy who was a real brute" he said. "No one ever did anything right. He was always finding fault. It was awful being on that ship. But, how can I get the crew to do their jobs without sounding too authoritarian?"

"The crew usually know their jobs, Richard" I said, "I'd let them perform and only comment if they do something wrong, and even then, there are ways of telling people how to do something."

I smiled at him.

"How did you get the way you are, Richard?" I smiled again "I mean the person you are, not that fancy uniform. Did anyone tell you what to do?"

He thought about that.

"No. I guess not. Not told anyway. Maybe a suggestion. But I had to do it myself, didn't I. Even make stupid mistakes like running away."

He looked at me again.

"Will I make a good leader, Ma'am?"

"The fact that you are so concerned means that you probably will" I answered.

He took a handful of peas and started eating them raw. "Is there any bread? I could do with a bread and peas sandwich."

Then he started to grin.

"Look, Ma'am. I'll be O.K. I know that. If I run into any problems I'll ask myself 'what would Ma'am do?' Maybe I'll even call. We've got phones, you know. I'll call her and say "Ma'am. Help. What do I do?"

"And what would I tell you?" I asked.

"Oh. The usual. What do you think?" he replied.

"I've got Unions, Shipping Companies, Crew, Longshoremen, all kinds of Port Authorities to contend with now. What a mess. And me who hated Bureaucracies."

Then he started to laugh.

"I hope that that baker knows how to make bread. This Captain is going to need a lot." And then, very seriously "Thanks Ma'am. I'll be O.K. You saw to that."

He sighed, got up from his chair, stood up.

"May I stay over? he asked "I'll drive to Boston early this morning."

"Of course" I replied "Always".

I heard him going up the stairs. Heard him say 'Hi Hank' and then it was quiet.

I finished freezing the peas and went upstairs. I tapped on his door.

"Come in" he said" I'm here."

He was sitting on the side of his bed. His uniform was neatly folded on the chair. His chest was bare and he only wore a pair of shorts.

He looked up as I came in.

"Ma'am" he said "I've been thinking."

"I thought that you were taking a nap" I said.

"No. Just thinking."

"Thinking?"

"How did you ever put up with me" he asked "A snotty, beligerent, dumb kid."

"Is that what you were?" I asked.

"Wasn't I" he asked.

"Not what I saw. I saw a very frightened, but loveable kid who needed a lot of loving."

"Well" he said "I guess you must have changed me somewhere. I was never that."

"Of course you were, Richard" I said "I never changed you. That kid is still you today. I just helped you get rid of the garbage."

"How?" he asked "How?"

"Unconditional love" I answered. "Look at Hank. He did not care that when you first came you stank of beer and were dirty. Even when he had to share your bed with all those chicks, those empty little girls you brought here, he still loved you. To him you were Richard, and he did not care beyond that."

"And you? he asked.

"Me too" I said.

"You know" he said "Speaking of beer. I wanted a beer so desperately that day, needed it, my body shrieked for beer, and you gave me chicken soup. Chicken soup does not taste like beer. And then you gave me bread. Something about it being good for seasick passengers, you said. I wasn't seasick. I never have been. But, I thought, I better chew it anyway. So every time I wanted a beer, I'd chew on a piece of bread. Cold Turkey. I nearly died that first couple of weeks. But after awhile beer became bread, and now I eat bread because it's bread."

"I know how you struggled" I told him. "It was part of our unspoken agreement, and I loved you and ached for you when I saw you struggle. But, you made it, Cold Turkey, and I was relieved and proud for you."

I went to his chest of drawers, pulled out an old T-shirt, one with a red cat on it, like Hank. "Here, put this on, even though it's June, it gets chilly."

He did so.

"Unconditionsl love" he mused "Did you always love me?"

"Always" I said "Even when I got so angry with you."

"Like when?" he questioned.

"Like when you told me you hated me, and I knew you were really fighting the love you were beginning to feel for me. Like when I'd see you trembling in fear because you were afraid of being beaten. Like your stupid argument about freedom. Like…" And then I saopped. "I can't think of anymore."

As I was speaking, I suddenly recalled something.

"Richard" I said "I'm glad that you never removed those scars. Remember that some of your crew may come from where you were. We are all capable of carrying scars, inner or outer. If you treat your men decently and fairly, and see them as people, not their scars, then you will be O.K. And remember, you could have been in their shoes very easily. It's only luck that helped you."

He looked at me and laughed.

"Lady luck" he said "A lucky lady called Ma'am."

He added.

"I've said it before. I'll say it again. Thanks Ma'a,. I hope that I've turned out to be the son that does not make his mother cry."

"Just remember" I said "Just be Richard. You'll be fine."

And I kissed him again. "Get dressed" I said "Let's have dinner."

Seafarer's families don't get to see their children very often.   We get gifts from everywhere, and via the grapevine, we hear about thre.

Since Richard's first ship, he has been on many others, and traveled to many different places.

From what I hear, he is respected by his crew, and they sign on, over and over, to be on his ship. His is a happy ship, and a well run one, and because Richard is so humane, so too, is his crew.

I receive letters and gifts from everywhere, and I have had my share of anxiety as well.

I try not to worry, but if letters are delayed I worry. If there is a storm, I worry. If I hear of accidents on ships, collisions or fires, I worry.

I try not to. I know thst Richard is a good seafarer and as competent as he can be in any circumstance.

John, who is not First Mate and sails with Richard, also writes and keeps me informed.

I save all the letters that I receive, and carefully label and date them as they come.

The two I prize most are the ones he sent me, the first after he signed on as Third Mate on his first ship so long ago, and the second, the one Richard wrote me after taking command of his first ship.

I reprint them here in full.

RICHARD

At sea

Hi Ma'am

This ship ain't no Bluenose. But she has all the qualities of one. You were right. She talks to me with every squeak and groan, and as long as I listen to her, I will be O.K.

The smell of sea, and tar and wood and oil reminds me so much of you.

So far I'm O.K. The meals are O.K. and they give me plenty of bread.

Take care of yourself and Hank for me.

Love

Richard

Mariam Ghose Sherar

Nearing Calcutta

Dear Ma'am

This ship is due in Calcutta tomorrow, and I hope to go ashore and visit your relatives, and mine.

The baker on this ship must think that his Captain is crazy. I have to have a fresh loaf of bread brought to me every morning.

Wherever I go, whatever I do, whatever I eat, I always carry bread with me. It symbolizes the life that you gave me when all I wanted was beer, and the nourishment I needed to heal those 'inner scars'.

Don't worry. I'm O.K. and I always will be.

I love you

Your son

Richard

About the Author

Mariam Ghose Sherar is a retired Professor of Sociology from Long Island University, Brooklyn, N.Y. Her interest has always been in the Social Problem and Maritime Sociology areas. Since retirement, she has translated these into novels, of which *Richard* is the first. In a world of violence and domestic abuse Mrs. Sherar pleads for peaceful solutions and strongly believes that unconditional love and belief in the individual can heal and restore youth to their full potential.

She has lived in India during her childhood and is a grandmother. She has one daughter Farida. She currently lives in Cherryfield, Maine and writes the weekly column for the Downeast Coastal Press.